EXPRESS

SOURCEBOOK

**Practice Workshops
and Minilessons
for the Proofreader's Guide**

TE

TEACHER'S EDITION · TEACHER'S EDITION

. . . a resource of student
workshops, minilessons, and
activities to accompany

WRITERS

EXPRESS

WRITE SOURCE®

GREAT SOURCE EDUCATION GROUP

a Houghton Mifflin Company
Wilmington, Massachusetts

A Few Words About the Level 5 SourceBook

Before you begin . . .

You need to know that the SourceBook should be used with the *Writers Express* handbook, which provides information, examples, and models. The SourceBook provides your students with opportunities to practice the editing and proofreading skills presented in the handbook. SourceBook activities are organized into Practice Workshops, Minilessons, and Check-It-Out Daily Sentences.

Practice Workshops

The Practice Workshops cover what students need to know to become better writers and proofreaders. The workshop topics appear in the same order in the SourceBook as they do in the Proofreader's Guide in the *Writers Express* handbook. In each workshop, The First Step introduces the basic idea and directs students to the handbook pages they will want to use. Each workshop has clear directions and examples. Follow-up writing activities are explained in The Next Step.

Minilessons

Each Minilesson covers one idea from the handbook. Most minilessons can be done individually or with a partner.

Check-It-Out Daily Sentences

Check-It-Out Daily Sentences review basic writing skills. Focused Sentences help your students concentrate on one editing skill at a time. Proofreading Sentences offer several different sentence problems for students to correct. Sometimes they will add a word, write a different word, or simply cross out a word. Such practice helps them become more careful writers and better proofreaders.

Authors: Pat Sebranek and Dave Kemper

Trademarks and trade names are shown in this book strictly for illustrative purposes and are the property of their respective owners. The authors' references herein should not be regarded as affecting their validity.

Printed in the United States of America

International Standard Book Number: 0-669-43696-8

5 6 7 8 9 10 -HLG- 02 01 00 99

Table of Contents

Sentence Workshops

Understanding Sentences

• Language Workshops

Understanding Our Language

• Minilessons

• Check-It-Out Sentences

Focused Sentences

• Check-It-Out Sentences

Proofreading Sentences

Practice Workshops

The activities in this section of the SourceBook cover the basic language, editing, and proofreading skills students need to become better writers.

End Punctuation 1

The First Step ● Choosing the correct **end punctuation** is a basic step in punctuating your writing. Your handbook explains when to use the three kinds of end punctuation: the period, the question mark, and the exclamation point. (See topic numbers 02, 54, and 56 in "Marking Punctuation," which starts on page 343.)

DIRECTIONS: **Put the correct end punctuation—a period, a question mark, or an exclamation point—in the sentences below. You will also need to capitalize the first letter of each sentence. The first sentence has been marked for you.**

H
*H*ave you ever wondered who the very first Americans were *?* *S*cientists say they came from Asia thousands of years ago *.* *A*t that time, land connected Asia to the part of North America that is now Alaska *.* *I*magine that *.*

*P*eople followed herds of animals across the "land bridge" between Asia and America *.* *T*hey needed these animals for food and clothing *.* *I*t was much too cold to grow crops *.* *T*he first Americans slowly moved farther and farther south *.* *A*fter thousands of years, people reached the tip of South America *.*

*C*an you imagine living in a cave in a place where it is cold and snowy all the time *?* *N*o wonder people headed south *.* *(or)* *!*

End Punctuation 1

The Next Step ● Write a paragraph describing your coldest experience. Try to use at least two words or phrases that might be followed by an exclamation point (Unbelievable!).

End Punctuation 2

> **The First Step** ● This activity gives you practice using correct **end punctuation**. Check your handbook (pages 343-351) if you need help with this activity.

DIRECTIONS: Put the correct end punctuation in the sentences below, and capitalize the first letter of each sentence. The first sentence has been marked for you.

T/the first superhero, Superman, came on the scene in 1938. *H*/he was created by a writer and an artist who lived in Ohio, and he was no average Joe. *H*/how fast was Superman? *H*/he was faster than a speeding bullet. *H*/he was also strong enough to bend steel with his bare hands. *H*/he had many special powers because he was from a planet called Krypton. *O*/of course, he always used his powers to fight evil.

Superman was so popular that he was in comic books and newspapers and on radio and TV. *W*/when World War II started, Superman had millions of fans. *H*/his creators had to decide whether Superman would join the army. *W*/what did they decide? *W*/well, Superman tried to join the army, but he failed his eye exam. *H*/how could that have happened? *H*/his X-ray vision caused him to read an eye chart in the next room, instead of the one he was supposed to read.

End Punctuation 2

The Next Step ● Write a brief story describing a battle between Superman and a force of evil. Use the three kinds of end punctuation in your story. (*Hint:* You should be able to use lots of exclamation points.)

Using Commas 1

The First Step ● **Commas** are used between words or phrases in a series. Commas are used between two independent clauses that are joined by words such as *and, but, or, so,* and *yet.* (See handbook page 345, topic numbers 12 and 16.)

Examples:

Commas in a Series

People who do well in sprints are fast**,** strong**,** and dedicated.

Comma Between Two Independent Clauses

I used to run sprints**,** but now I am much more interested in the long jump.

DIRECTIONS: In the paragraph below, add commas between independent clauses and between items in a series. The first sentence has been marked for you.

Jessie Owens was a track star in the 1930's**,** and he was an African-American. He set six world records in 1935**,** and the next year he won four gold medals at the Olympics in Germany. Adolf Hitler, the German dictator, was a bigot**,** so he didn't like the fact that Jesse Owens was the star of the Olympics. Owens also faced prejudice**,** disappointment**,** and unkindness in the United States. He had won four gold medals**,** yet the award for best American athlete of the year was given to a white man who had won only one medal. However, a huge, noisy parade was held for Owens in New York City**,** and someone threw a small, closed, white bag into his car. He thought there were cookies in the bag**,** but he opened it and found $10,000 in cash!

Using Commas 2

The First Step ● **Commas** are used between words or phrases in a series and between two independent clauses that are joined by words such as *and*, *but*, or *so*. Commas are also used between items in dates. (See handbook page 345 and the examples below.)

Commas in a Series

The national anthem is as American as red**,** white**,** and blue.

Comma Between Two Independent Clauses

I know the words to "The Star-Spangled Banner**,**" but I can't hit all the notes! (**Note**: The comma is placed inside the quotation marks.)

Commas Between Items in Dates

I first heard the national anthem at a baseball game on July 4**,** 1988.

DIRECTIONS: In the paragraph below, add commas between independent clauses, between items in a series, and between items in dates. The first sentence has been marked for you.

Americans have been singing "The Star-Spangled Banner" since the early 1800's**,** but it wasn't our official national anthem until 1931. On November 3**,** 1929**,** newspapers printed the news that there was no official anthem. Five million people wrote to ask Congress to choose one**,** but many of them didn't want "The Star-Spangled Banner." Some people didn't like the fact that the music was written in England. After all, we had fought against England for our freedom. But the music to "Yankee Doodle**,**" "Hail to the Chief**,**" and other songs is also from England! "America the Beautiful**,**" "America**,**" and a few others received votes**,** but "The Star-Spangled Banner" won the day.

Using Commas 3

The First Step ● Commas *again!* Well, commas are important! You'll be using them for the rest of your life, so it's important to use them right! Remember to check your handbook if you're not sure when or how to use commas. (See handbook page 345, topic numbers 12, 13, and 16.)

DIRECTIONS: In the paragraph below, add commas between independent clauses, between items in a series, and between items in dates. The first sentence has been marked for you.

Henry Ford invented the first mass-produced car, and he called it the Model T. The Model T was a big success, but Henry Ford didn't stop there. On December 2, 1927, a new model was introduced. Many people were curious about the new Model A, so they flocked to see it. In Cleveland, police on horseback had to keep the huge, excited crowds in line. So that everyone could see it, the Model A was placed on a high platform in Kansas City. Ford salespeople said that the Model A rode smoothly, gave a fast ride, and was dependable. They also claimed that it had been clocked at 71 miles per hour! Every Model T was black, but the new Model A came in new, exciting colors such as Arabian Sand and Niagara Blue.

Using Commas 3

The Next Step ● Write a basic news story announcing the development of a new car. Tell what makes the car special. Use commas correctly! (See pages 128-129 for help with your writing.)

10 *Marking Punctuation*

Punctuating Appositives

The First Step ● As you know by now, commas are used in many different ways. This time, you're going to practice using commas to set off **appositives**. An appositive is a word or phrase that *renames* or *explains* the noun that comes before. (See your handbook, page 346, topic number 22.)

DIRECTIONS: Use commas to set off the appositives in the following sentences. The first two have been done for you.

1. Mrs. Chang, our teacher, won an award.

2. The award, a gift certificate, was for being an excellent teacher.

3. Our principal, Mrs. Greene, presented the award.

4. Mrs. Chang, the best teacher I've had yet, deserved to win.

5. Alisha, who is in our class, read a poem about Mrs. Chang.

6. Mrs. Chang's husband, a math teacher, was there.

7. The rest of us sang a song, "You're the Best," for Mrs. Chang.

8. Bobby, who wants to be a musician, wrote the song.

9. Tamara, a computer whiz, made a banner on her computer.

10. The banner, six feet long, said, "Way to go, Mrs. Chang!"

Punctuating Appositives

The Next Step ● Write four sentences, each one saying something about a different person you know. Start each sentence with a person's name, then add an appositive that tells something about the person, and then finish the sentence. Use commas correctly!

1. _____

_____

_____

2. _____

_____

_____

3. _____

_____

_____

4. _____

_____

_____

Commas Between Clauses

The First Step ● Here's another place where **commas** signal readers to pause: after a long phrase or clause that introduces the rest of the sentence. Check out your handbook, page 346, topic number 23.

DIRECTIONS: In each of the following sentences, place a comma after the introductory phrase or clause. The first one has been done for you.

1. Invented by a British blacksmith in 1839, the bicycle became the world's most popular form of transportation.

2. Long before batteries or electricity, a Greek inventor made a clock that was powered by moving water.

3. Better known as an astronomer, Galileo invented the thermometer.

4. About 7,500 years ago in Turkey, people used a natural glass called obsidian for mirrors.

5. A year before Thomas Edison introduced his light bulb, a British inventor made one.

6. When the first movie was shown, people fainted because they thought the train in the movie would run over them!

7. Although we don't think of it as such, paper is an invention.

8. Invented in China in the year 105, paper is now used all over the world.

Name _____

Commas and End Punctuation Review

The First Step ● This workshop activity is a review of commas and end punctuation. (See topic numbers 02, 54, 56, 12, and 16 in "Marking Punctuation," which begins on page 343 in your handbook.)

DIRECTIONS: Add needed commas and end punctuation marks in the sentences below. Also capitalize the first letter of each new sentence. The first sentence has been done for you.

In the early 1800's only about half of the kids in the United States went to school. many people thought that only boys should go to school, so girls were usually not allowed to attend. a few special teachers thought that American schools should be open to girls, too.

Sara Pierce started a school for girls, and she taught grammar, reading, writing, and history. one of her students was Harriet Beecher Stowe. ms. Stowe later wrote a famous novel called *Uncle Tom's Cabin*. the first college to accept women was Mount Holyoke College, and it was started by Mary Lyon. Emily Dickinson, another great writer, was a student there.

one teacher became famous for writing books for both boys and girls. he wrote the first American dictionary, and his name is still on many dictionaries. can you guess his name? sure you can. his name was Noah Webster.

Using Semicolons

The First Step ● **Semicolons** can be confusing. What do they mean? What are you supposed to do with them? Well, first read about them on page 347 in your handbook. Then get some hands-on practice by doing these activities.

DIRECTIONS: Each sentence below contains two independent clauses that are separated by a conjunction and a comma. Cross out the conjunction and comma, and use a semicolon to separate the independent clauses instead. The first sentence has been marked for you.

Roy C. Sullivan was a park ranger, but his life was more exciting than you might think. He was struck by lightning seven times, but he lived to tell about it. No one understood why Sullivan kept getting hit by lightning, and it's amazing that he kept working! Lightning "fired" several of his hats, and one time it set fire to his hair.

The Next Step ● Semicolons are used to separate a series of phrases that contain commas. (See handbook page 347, topic number 26.) Write a sentence using the second set of phrases below.

buy cat food, cat toys, and litter ■ clean the cat box, hallway, and closet ■ give Fuzzball a good brushing

Example: I'm supposed to buy cat food, cat toys, and litter; clean the cat box, hallway, and closet; and give Fuzzball a good brushing.

see the lions, tigers, and bears ■ eat hot dogs, ice cream, and cotton candy ■ walk home in time for supper

Mario wants to see the lions, tigers, and bears; eat hot dogs, ice cream, and cotton candy; and walk home in time for supper.

Using Hyphens

> **The First Step** ● **Hyphens** are explained on page 348 in your handbook. The following two activities give you practice using them.

Using Hyphens to Join

DIRECTIONS: Put hyphens where they are needed in the sentences below. The first sentence has been marked for you.

1. Mom puts big pieces of chocolate in her chocolate-chunk cookies.

2. The governor-elect has a lot to learn about her new job.

3. My great-grandfather was a well-known doctor.

4. I once made a long-distance call to Japan.

5. My sister chews sugar-free gum.

6. I have an eight-year-old cousin who looks like me.

Using Hyphens to Divide

DIRECTIONS: Use hyphens to divide the following words into syllables.

1. contents   _con-tents_
2. writing   _writ-ing_
3. item   _i-tem_
4. revise   _re-vise_
5. improving   _im-prov-ing_

6. history   _his-to-ry_
7. connection   _con-nec-tion_
8. arithmetic   _a-rith-me-tic_
9. vocabulary   _vo-cab-u-la-ry_
10. apostrophe   _a-pos-tro-phe_

> **The Next Step** ● Check your work by looking up each word in a dictionary. It will show you how to divide words into syllables.

Using Apostrophes 1

The First Step ● **Apostrophes** are sometimes used to show possession, other times to make contractions. There's a lot to learn about apostrophes. Start by reading page 349 in your handbook!

DIRECTIONS: In the following paragraph, use apostrophes to make as many contractions as you can. The first one has been made for you.

Jessica *doesn't* ~~does not~~ like to sit in class on warm spring days. *She'd* She would rather be out playing baseball with Jose and Jennifer. *They're* They are all baseball nuts. *They'll* They will spend all summer playing baseball, *I'm* I am sure. Jessica always says *it's* it is too nice to be inside, even if *it's* it is raining. I like baseball, too, but I *don't* do not want to play in the rain. On rainy days, I *I'd* would rather play computer games.

DIRECTIONS: In this paragraph, add apostrophes where they are needed to form possessives. The first one has been done for you. (You will add six apostrophes.)

From the age of 11, Clara Barton's goal was to be a nurse. Her brothers' illness showed her that she liked to help sick people. Later, with her father's permission, she went to help soldiers in the Civil War. Often she stood by a doctor's side as bullets whizzed by. At the war's end, she joined the International Red Cross. Later Barton crossed the Atlantic to help feed Russia's starving people during a famine. Clara Barton will always be remembered for her unselfish devotion to the world's people.

Using Apostrophes 1

The Next Step ● Use the possessive form of each of the following words in interesting or entertaining sentences. (See page 349 for help.)

1. handbook

_____

_____

_____

2. desk

_____

_____

_____

3. Mr. or Ms. _____ (your principal's name)

_____

_____

4. _____ (your name)

_____

_____

_____

Using Apostrophes 2

The First Step ● Think of this exercise as advanced **apostrophe** practice. To get ready, review page 349 in your handbook.

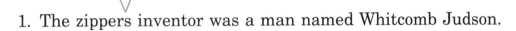

DIRECTIONS: Add apostrophes as needed in the sentences below. You'll use them to punctuate contractions, possessives, and plurals; and in place of numbers and letters.

1. The zippers inventor was a man named Whitcomb Judson.

2. Judsons idea was to use zippers to fasten boots.

3. But in 1918, the Navy used Judsons invention to fasten flight suits.

4. It wasnt called a zipper until 26.

5. The name "zipper" stuck in peoples minds, and soon zippers were everywhere.

6. The submarines inventor was David Bushnell, an American.

7. He built the first sub, but he didnt ride in it!

8. He didnt know whether it would work.

9. The first subs mission was to attack a British ship in 1776.

10. The sub, called the *Turtle*, wasnt able to sink the ship.

11. Most people know about the Wright brothers invention, the airplane.

12. It took off in 1903, but the first helicopter didnt fly until 1907.

13. Blaise Pascals famous invention is the calculator.

14. You might say that a calculator is an invention that has its +s and −s.

Using Apostrophes 2

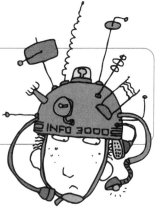

The Next Step ● Review the inventions listed in the handbook (pages 430-439). Write about one of these inventions in a paragraph. Use at least two possessives and two contractions. (Have a classmate check your work.)

_____

_____

_____

_____

_____

_____

_____

_____

_____

_____

_____

_____

_____

_____

Using Quotation Marks 1

The First Step ● What do **quotation marks** mark? They mark the exact words a person speaks. They are also used to mark the titles of songs, poems, short stories, articles, etc. (See page 350 in your handbook for more information about quotation marks.)

DIRECTIONS: Add quotation marks where they are needed in the following sentences. The first two sentences have been marked for you.

1. Ricardo said, "I'm going to the library. Do you want to come?"

2. "No," I answered. "But will you check out a book for me?"

3. "Sure," Ricardo said. "What book do you want?"

4. I asked him to bring me any book that included Edgar Allen Poe's poem called "The Raven."

5. "That's a great poem," Ricardo said. He asked me if I had read any of his other poems, such as "The Bells" and "Annabel Lee."

6. I told him I hadn't read any of Poe's poems yet, but I had to read "The Raven" for class.

7. "No problem. I'm sure I can find it," he said. "Do you want anything else?"

8. "No, thanks," I said. "If Poe's poems are like his short stories, I'll be too scared to read anything else!"

The Next Step ● Re-create a conversation you and a friend have had about school, sports, books or movies. Be sure to use quotation marks correctly.

Using Quotation Marks 2

The First Step ● **Quotation marks** are used to set off dialogue. (See handbook page 350 and the student model "The Vacation" on page 165.)

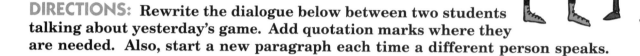

DIRECTIONS: Rewrite the dialogue below between two students talking about yesterday's game. Add quotation marks where they are needed. Also, start a new paragraph each time a different person speaks.

Did you see the game yesterday? Rodrigo shouted as he jogged up the steps leading to the art room. Yeah, wasn't it great! Maria shouted back. I didn't think we had a chance. I mean, two goals to zero with only two minutes . . . ! I know! Rodrigo interrupted. I switched the channel twice before I realized what was happening. What a rally! Now it's the semifinals against Brazil, whispered Maria as they headed for their seats in the front row.

"Did you see the game yesterday?" Rodrigo shouted as he jogged up the steps leading to the art room.

"Yeah, wasn't it great!" Maria shouted back. "I didn't think we had a chance. I mean, two goals to zero with only two minutes . . . !"

"I know!" Rodrigo interrupted. "I switched the channel twice before I realized what was happening. What a rally!"

"Now it's the semifinals against Brazil," whispered Maria as they headed for their seats in the front row.

Using Quotation Marks 3

The First Step ● **Quotation marks** are used in exactly the same way when quoting written or spoken words. (See handbook page 350, topic numbers 49-50.)

DIRECTIONS: Below are some quotes from famous books. Add quotation marks where they are needed. The first one has been done for you.

1. In *A Christmas Carol*, Charles Dickens wrote, "Scrooge looked about him for the ghost, and saw it not."

2. "Rip's story was soon told, for the whole 20 years had been to him but as one night," wrote Washington Irving in "Rip Van Winkle."

3. Mark Twain wrote, in *The Adventures of Huckleberry Finn*, "We went to a clump of bushes, and Tom made everybody swear to keep the secret, and then showed them a hole in the hill, right in the thickest part of the bushes."

4. "At last he heard along the road at the foot of the hill the clatter of a horse's galloping hoofs," wrote Stephen Crane in *The Red Badge of Courage*.

5. In "The Legend of Sleepy Hollow," Washington Irving wrote, "The night grew darker and darker; the stars seemed to sink deeper in the sky, and driving clouds occasionally hid them from his sight."

Using Quotation Marks 3

_____

_____

_____

_____

_____

_____

_____

_____

_____

_____

_____

_____

_____

Punctuating Titles

The First Step ● When you include a **title** in your writing, how do you punctuate it? The general rule is that titles of complete works (such as books) are italicized, while titles of parts of works (such as book chapters) are put in quotation marks.

Page 350 in your handbook (topic number 52) explains which titles need quotation marks. Page 351 (topic number 58) explains which titles should be italicized.

DIRECTIONS: In the following sentences, put quotation marks around the titles that need them, and underline the titles that should be in italic type. The first sentence has been done for you.

1. "Too Many Cats!" is a story in a book called Cat Tales.

2. The Lion King and Aladdin are Disney movies.

3. Our science book has chapters called "The Planets and Beyond" and "Rivers and Seas."

4. Part of a poem called "The New Colossus" by Emma Lazarus is written on the Statue of Liberty.

5. Little Richard sings "Old MacDonald" on his kids' album called Shake It All About.

6. Mom likes to watch The Simpsons.

7. My dad reads two newspapers, the Atlanta Constitution and the Wall Street Journal, plus Time magazine.

Punctuating Titles

The Next Step ● Write five sentences, each one including one of the following titles: your favorite song, album, TV show, movie, and book. Punctuate the titles correctly.

1. (song)

_____

_____

2. (album)

_____

_____

3. (TV show)

_____

_____

4. (movie)

_____

_____

5. (book)

_____

_____

Using Italics and Parentheses

The First Step ● **Italics** and **parentheses** are explained on page 351 in your handbook. This activity gives you some practice using these special punctuation marks.

DIRECTIONS: In the following sentences, underline all titles that should be in italics, and add parentheses where they are needed. The first sentence has been marked for you.

1. Washington Irving wrote a book of stories called The Sketch Book. Rip Van Winkle (he's the guy who slept for 20 years) is a character in one of Irving's stories.

2. Phillis Wheatley was a slave (she was brought to America when she was about seven) and never went to school. But she wrote poetry that was published in The London Magazine.

3. James Fenimore Cooper wrote both stories (one book of stories is called The Leather-Stocking Tales) and novels. His novel The Last of the Mohicans was made into a movie.

4. Early American writers created a new kind of story, the tall tale, about larger-than-life heroes (Paul Bunyan and Pecos Bill are examples).

5. Louisa May Alcott wrote a book about her family (it's called Little Women) and became a favorite author of many young readers.

Using Italics and Parentheses

The Next Step ● Write sentences for each of the titles listed below. Use parentheses at least once in each sentence. Also make sure to underline words that should be in italics.

1. *Writers Express* (book)

_____

_____

_____

2. *The Lion King* (movie)

_____

_____

_____

3. *Guinness Book of Records* (book)

_____

_____

_____

4. *Sports Illustrated for Kids* (magazine)

_____

_____

_____

Punctuation Review

The First Step ● This paragraph uses almost all the different kinds of punctuation you've practiced so far. Use "Marking Punctuation" on pages 343-351 in your handbook to help you.

DIRECTIONS: Punctuation marks are missing from each of the following sentences. Correct the sentences by adding commas, apostrophes, semicolons, hyphens, and end punctuation. The first sentence has been marked for you.

The game of Monopoly is popular now, but it didn't start out that way. Charles Darrow, the inventor, tried to sell the game to Parker Brothers Company, but they didn't want to buy it. Parker Brothers said Darrow's game took too long to play, had mistakes in the instructions, and wouldn't sell. Darrow had a few Monopoly games made, and he paid for them himself. Monopoly became very popular, so Parker Brothers decided to buy it after all. Monopoly became the best-selling game of all time; more Monopoly money than real money is printed every year. How do you think Charles Darrow would have felt about this?

Punctuation Review

The Next Step ● Write a paragraph about your favorite game. Explain why you like the game, why you are good at it, and so on. Trade paragraphs with a classmate when you are done. Carefully check each other's work for punctuation.

Capitalization 1

The First Step ● You already know that the first letter of a sentence is always **capitalized**. And you probably know that proper nouns are capitalized. But, uh, what's a proper noun? Glad you asked. This activity gives you practice with proper nouns.

DIRECTIONS: Your handbook explains the rules for capitalization on pages 352-354. Use topic numbers 63, 65, 67, and 71 to find and change the words that should be capitalized. The first sentence has been marked for you.

1. Gustavo and I went with ᴰd̸ad to meet ᴳg̸overnor ꟻf̸lood.

2. He came to our town to give a speech about ᴹm̸ayor ꟻf̸rost.

3. We live in ᴿr̸agener, ˢs̸outh ᶜc̸arolina.

4. The governor doesn't come here very often, ᴰd̸ad says, but ᴹm̸ayor ꟻf̸rost is a friend of his.

5. So, he came from the capital city, ᶜc̸olumbia, to give a speech in honor of the mayor.

6. According to ᴹm̸om, ᴳg̸overnor ꟻf̸lood would go all the way to ᴹm̸ars for ᴹm̸ayor ꟻf̸rost.

7. According to ᴰd̸ad, the governor would rather go to ᵂw̸ashington, ᴰ·ᶜ·d̸c, than to ᴹm̸ars.

8. He thinks ᴳg̸overnor ꟻf̸lood wants to be president someday.

Capitalization 1

The Next Step ● Write a paragraph about a speech, game, concert, or other event you have attended. (Or, write about one you'd *like* to attend!) Include as much information as you can about when and where it was; what well-known people, teams, or performers you saw; etc. Be sure to capitalize correctly!

Capitalization 2

The First Step ● Your handbook lists 14 different rules for **capitalization**. (See pages 352-354.) That's a lot of rules to learn! In this activity, most of the practice is on topic numbers 68, 70, 75, and 76. But you'll need to use a few others, too.

DIRECTIONS: Each of the following sentences contains two or more capitalization errors. Some words and phrases that *should* be capitalized are not; some words and phrases that *should not* be capitalized are. Make the needed corrections. The first sentence has been done for you.

1. My grandfather fought in the *K*orean *W*ar and in *W*orld *W*ar II.

2. In history class, we're studying the *R*evolutionary *W*ar and the first *p*resident of the United States.

3. The *L*eague of *N*ations was replaced by the *U*nited *N*ations.

4. I've seen the California *A*ngels play *b*aseball in Anaheim Stadium.

5. The most common religion in *J*apan is *B*uddhism.

6. Our *P*uerto *R*ican neighbors speak *S*panish at home.

7. Most people prefer either *C*oca-*C*ola or *P*epsi soft drinks.

8. Jay got a McDonald's *h*amburger and *B*urger *K*ing fries.

9. Jonathan is *J*ewish, and his family celebrates *H*anukkah.

10. Jamila, who is from *K*enya, knows how to speak *S*wahili.

11. The Flintstones lived in the *S*tone *A*ge, and the Jetsons lived in the *S*pace *A*ge.

Capitalization 2

The Next Step ● Choose any four of the rules for capitalization shown on handbook page 353. Then write four sentences. Each one of your sentences should use a different rule, but don't capitalize any words in your sentences. Trade with a partner, and correct each other's sentences. Write down the numbers of the rules you used to make the corrections.

Using Plurals

The First Step ● Page 355 in your handbook explains **plurals** and the rules for making them. Open your handbook to that page and do this activity.

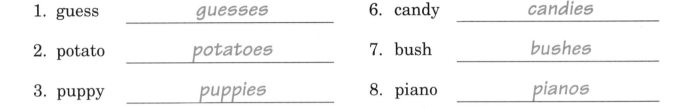

DIRECTIONS: Change each word into its plural form. Use the rules explained in topic numbers 78, 79, and 82 in your handbook.

1. guess   *guesses*
2. potato   *potatoes*
3. puppy   *puppies*
4. lunch   *lunches*
5. tomato   *tomatoes*

6. candy   *candies*
7. bush   *bushes*
8. piano   *pianos*
9. key   *keys*
10. box   *boxes*

The Next Step ● Now develop a "Found Poem," using as many of these words and their plural forms as possible. (See the model on page 204 in your handbook.)

(Answers will vary.)

Using Numbers

> **The First Step** ● This activity gives you practice using **numbers** in your writing. Page 356 in your handbook explains the rules for when to write numbers as numerals and when to write them as words.

DIRECTIONS: In the sentences below, all the numbers are written as words. Some of them should be written as numerals. Open your handbook to page 356. Using the rules in topic numbers 85, 87, and 88, find the numbers that should be written as numerals, and change them.

1. There are ~~eleven~~ *11* parts in the school play.

2. We also need about ~~ten~~ *10* people to sing in the chorus.

3. In the play, there are kids who are ~~five~~ *5* and ~~fifteen~~ *15 (either is correct)* years old; all the other parts are for adults.

4. Three people are needed to make costumes, and all ~~thirty~~ *30* of us involved with the play will sell tickets.

5. If we sell tickets for ~~three dollars~~ *$3.00 (or) $3* each, we'll have to sell ~~fifty~~ *50* tickets to pay for the costumes.

6. We could sell popcorn for ~~one dollar~~ *$1.00 (or) $1*, if two people will agree to sell it.

7. We plan to give the play on February ~~six~~ *6*, ~~seven~~ *7*, and ~~eight~~ *8* at ~~seven~~ *7:00 (or) 7* p.m.

> **The Next Step** ● Write two sentences that use numbers written correctly as numerals, and two sentences that use numbers written correctly as words.

Using Abbreviations

The First Step ● An **abbreviation** is a shorter way to write a word or phrase—a shortcut! Pages 356 and 357 in your handbook explain abbreviations and give examples.

DIRECTIONS: Below are some abbreviations that are often used in writing addresses and times. Match each abbreviation to the word or phrase it stands for.

   _c_   1. St.   a. ante meridiem (before noon)

   _f_   2. Ave.   b. Drive

   _g_   3. Rd.   c. Street

   _a_   4. a.m.   d. South

   _e_   5. p.m.   e. post meridiem (after noon)

   _b_   6. Dr.   f. Avenue

   _d_   7. S.   g. Road

DIRECTIONS: Below are some other common abbreviations. Match each abbreviation to the word or phrase it stands for.

   _b_   1. lb   a. Doctor of Medicine

   _d_   2. oz   b. pound

   _g_   3. etc.   c. paid

   _c_   4. pd.   d. ounce

   _a_   5. M.D.   e. Missus

   _f_   6. Ms.   f. combination of Miss and Missus

   _e_   7. Mrs.   g. et cetera (and so forth)

Using Abbreviations

The Next Step ● Now choose any four of the abbreviations from the matching lists and use them in sentences. You may use more than one abbreviation in a sentence.

Becoming a Better Speller

The First Step ● Making up sayings and acrostics can help you remember the spellings of difficult words. (See the bottom half of handbook page 271 for examples.)

DIRECTIONS: Try writing sayings or acrostics for four words from your spelling dictionary, or choose words that give you trouble from the list beginning on page 358. The first one has been done as an example.

(Answers will vary.)

1. *Their, there, and they're all begin with "the."*
_____
_____

2. _____
_____
_____

3. _____
_____
_____

4. _____
_____
_____

5. _____
_____

Becoming a Better Speller

The Next Step ● Share your sayings and acrostics with your group. Choose the best examples of each and write them below. (Your group might also make a spelling poster with the best sayings and acrostics on it.)

_____

_____

_____

_____

_____

_____

_____

_____

_____

_____

_____

_____

_____

Using the Right Word 1

The First Step ● Your handbook lists many of the words that are commonly misused in writing. (See pages 362-369.) Use this section to help you complete this workshop activity.

DIRECTIONS: Carefully read the following story. If an underlined word is incorrect, cross it out and write the correct form above it. If the underlined word is correct, leave it alone. The first two have been corrected for you. (Work on this activity with a partner if your teacher allows it.)

In 1849, the Riker family left ~~there~~ *their* home in the East to start a ~~knew~~ *new* life

in Oregon. Most pioneers traveled with other families because ~~their~~ *there* was

safety in numbers. But Janette Riker, her ~~too~~ *two* brothers, and their father

~~choose~~ *chose* to make the trip alone.

One day, when they were in Montana, the men went hunting. They never

came back. Janette was left alone in the wilderness. She ~~new~~ *knew* she would ~~dye~~ *die*

if she tried to cross the Rocky Mountains <u>by</u> herself.

Since cold ~~whether~~ *weather* was coming, Janette built a hut and chopped wood

~~four~~ *for* a fire. She even killed an ox <u>so</u> she would have ~~meet~~ *meat*. She ~~herd~~ *heard* wolves

and mountain lions sniffing at the door at ~~knight~~ *night*. Can you imagine spending

~~weak~~ *week* after ~~weak~~ *week* alone in a tiny hut, ~~weighting~~ *waiting* for spring?

When winter had ~~past~~ *passed*, Indians found Janette and

~~lead~~ *led* her to Oregon. They were surprised that she

lived ~~threw~~ *through* the winter!

Using the Right Word 1

The Next Step ● Here's your chance to see how well you understand the word pairs you just studied. Use the following pairs correctly in sentences. The first one has been done for you.

1. their, there

   Their new car is parked over there.

   _____

2. new, knew

   _____

   _____

3. choose, chose

   _____

   _____

4. passed, past

   _____

   _____

5. led, lead

   _____

   _____

Using the Right Word 2

The First Step ● Your handbook lists many of the words that are commonly misused in writing. (See pages 362-369.) Use this section to help you complete this workshop activity.

DIRECTIONS: If an underlined word is incorrect, cross it out and write the correct form above it. If the underlined word is correct, leave it alone. The first two have been corrected for you.

When settlers from Europe came to America, they had *a lot* ~~alot~~ to learn.

There were *no* ~~know~~ stores where they could *buy* ~~by~~ things. They had to *raise* ~~rays~~ crops

and hunt for food. Native Americans *knew* ~~new~~ all about the land and the animals,

so ~~sew~~ they <u>taught</u> the settlers about their new country.

Native Americans *taught* ~~learned~~ the settlers to catch fish from the rivers and

creeks ~~creaks~~. They told the settlers that when they planted corn, they should put a

small fish in the *hole* ~~whole~~ with the seeds. It didn't make any sense to the

settlers, but they tried it anyway. It worked! The corn plants produced more

ears of corn. The settlers also <u>learned</u> to hunt for *deer* ~~dear~~ and other animals.

They didn't <u>waste</u> anything: they *ate* ~~eight~~ the meat and used the *fur* ~~fir~~ to make

warm *clothes* ~~close~~.

America was full of things that the settlers had not <u>seen</u> in the *past* ~~passed~~.

They had never seen a *herd* ~~heard~~ of buffalo or *an* ~~a~~ eagle or eaten peanuts or

cranberries. America *seemed* ~~seamed~~ like a whole new world to them.

Using the Right Word 2

The Next Step ● Now test yourself by writing five sentences. Use the words listed below correctly in each sentence. The first one has been done for you.

1. raise

   The settlers learned to raise many new crops.

2. learned

3. creak

4. seam

5. heard

Name

Using the Right Word 3

The First Step ● Your handbook lists many of the words that are commonly misused in writing. (See pages 362-369.) Use this section to help you complete this workshop activity.

DIRECTIONS: If an underlined word is incorrect, cross it out and write the correct form above it. If the underlined word is correct, leave it alone. The first underlined word has been corrected for you.

The first Chinese immigrants came ~~too~~ _to_ America in the mid-1800's. They

were gold ~~minors~~ _miners_ in California. Soon, more Chinese people came to cook and

wash <u>clothes</u> for the miners. And about 10,000 Chinese men helped build ~~an~~ _a_

railroad that crossed the country from east to west.

At first, the Chinese were ~~excepted~~ _accepted_. But many miners didn't ~~fined~~ _find_ gold.

And ~~sum~~ _some_ people blamed the Chinese. When times get tough, ~~its~~ _it's_ easy to blame

people who are "new" or "different." Chinese men wore their ~~hare~~ _hair_ in long

braids, spoke a different language, and ~~eight~~ _ate_ different food <u>than</u> other

Americans. A few people wanted the Chinese and other immigrants to leave

~~there~~ _their_ new country because of such differences.

Many Chinese people stayed in America rather ~~then~~ _than_ give in to narrow-

minded people. Today, <u>they're</u> part of ~~hour~~ _our_ nation,

along with people from every other country in the

world.

Using the Right Word 3

The Next Step ● Write sentences in which you use each of the following words correctly. Exchange your sentences with a partner and check each other's work.

1. past

_____

_____

2. minors

_____

_____

3. than

_____

_____

4. their

_____

_____

5. through

_____

_____

Changing Sentence Beginnings

The First Step ● When you polish your writing, one thing to check is how your sentences start. If they all start the same way, your writing will be boring. Read **Change Your Sentence Beginnings** on page 51 in your handbook for ideas.

DIRECTIONS: In the following paragraph, all the sentences start exactly the same way. Using the ideas you found in your handbook, rewrite the paragraph so that most of the sentences have different beginnings. (You can leave one or two the way they are.) The first sentence has been rewritten for you as an example.

Evan leaves a trail of trouble even when he isn't trying. Evan and I were painting pictures at the kitchen table the last time I baby-sat for him. Evan painted a couple of monster faces, and then decided he wanted to do something else. Evan even offered to help clean up, which surprised me a little. Evan was carrying the bowl full of dirty water from our paintbrushes when disaster struck. Evan tripped right in front of the sink in the utility room, and the dirty water went flying. Evan will never be allowed to help again, I reminded myself as I worked.

Even when he isn't trying, Evan leaves a trail of trouble.

(Answers will vary.)

The Next Step ● Turn to page 63 in your handbook and read the model narrative paragraph. How is your rewritten paragraph different? Which do you like better?

Using Powerful Words

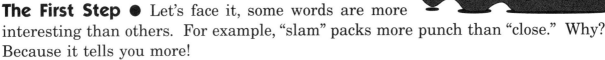

The First Step ● Let's face it, some words are more interesting than others. For example, "slam" packs more punch than "close." Why? Because it tells you more!

Interesting words are one Texas-size step toward interesting writing. On page 52 in your handbook, you'll find more about using **power-packed words**.

DIRECTIONS: Rewrite the following sentences, replacing the underlined words with more powerful words or phrases. If you have trouble coming up with words, ask yourself: What kind of person or thing was it? What did it look like, or sound like, or taste like? How did the action happen? Be creative! The first sentence has been done for you.

(Answers will vary.)

1. I told the dog to stop biting on my shoes!

   I screamed at the Doberman to stop chomping on my tennis shoes!

2. That dog was dumb.

   _____

3. The door came open, and a man walked in.

   _____

4. Sam ate his food and left.

   _____

5. The big trees cast big, dark shadows.

   _____

6. The cookies tasted good.

   _____

7. My sister drove Dad's car into a ditch.

   _____

8. Someone sent my mom some pretty flowers.

   _____

Simple Subjects and Simple Verbs

The First Step ● What are the two basic parts that every sentence must have? Right: a subject and a verb. Your handbook explains them on pages 86 and 371.

DIRECTIONS: Open your handbook to page 125. Look at the model newspaper story, "Jaws!" The last paragraph has five sentences. Find the subject in each sentence. Then rewrite the sentences, changing the subject. The new subject can be anything you choose, as long as it makes a correct sentence. The first sentence has been done for you as an example.

Important Note: The last two sentences are compound sentences, so they each have two subjects. In each sentence, pick just *one* of the two subjects to change.

(Answers will vary.)

1. *The raccoon swam back to the shore.*

2. _____

3. _____

4. _____

5. _____

Simple Subjects and Simple Verbs

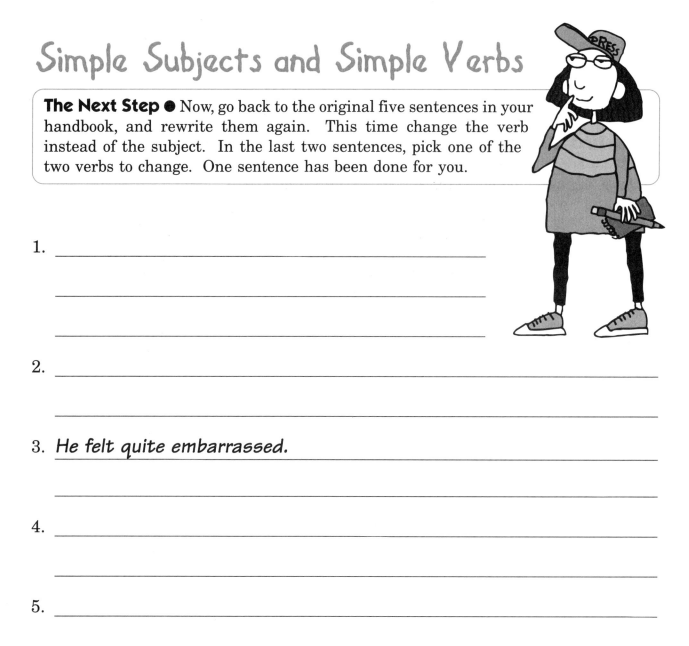

The Next Step ● Now, go back to the original five sentences in your handbook, and rewrite them again. This time change the verb instead of the subject. In the last two sentences, pick one of the two verbs to change. One sentence has been done for you.

1. _____

_____

_____

2. _____

_____

3. *He felt quite embarrassed.* _____

_____

4. _____

_____

5. _____

_____

Fixing Fragments 1

The First Step ● Your handbook explains different kinds of sentence errors and how to correct them. (See handbook page 87.) This activity gives you practice correcting one kind of sentence error, **sentence fragments**.

DIRECTIONS: On each line below, put an **S** if the words that follow make a sentence, or an **F** if they are a fragment. For each fragment, figure out what is missing—the subject or the verb—and write that word on the line to the right of the fragment. The first fragment has been marked for you.

_F___ 1. a baby alligator to our science class _____**verb**_____

_F___ 2. brought it from the zoo _____*subject*_____

_S___ 3. it was only about one foot long _____

_F___ 4. named her Alice _____*subject*_____

_F___ 5. was afraid of the alligator _____*subject*_____

_F___ 6. Alice afraid of him, too _____*verb*_____

_S___ 7. next week the zookeeper will bring another animal _____

_F___ 8. our teacher animals _____*verb*_____

Fixing Fragments 1

The Next Step ● Go back to the fragments on page 51 and make them into complete sentences. Add a subject or a verb, whichever is needed. Use correct capitalization and punctuation. The first one has been done for you.

(Answers may vary.)

1. **A baby alligator <u>came</u> to our science class.**

2. The zookeeper brought it from the zoo.

3. We named her Alice.

4. Alex was afraid of the alligator.

5. Alice was afraid of him, too.

6. Our teacher loves animals.

Fixing Fragments 2

The First Step ● This activity gives you practice correcting **sentence fragments**.

DIRECTIONS: On each line below, put an **S** if the words that follow make a sentence. Put an **F** if they are a fragment. For each fragment, figure out what is missing—the subject or the verb—and write that word on the line to the right of the fragment. The first one has been done for you.

_F_	1. Franklin Roosevelt president from 1933 to 1945	**verb**
_F_	2. was elected four times	_subject_
_S_	3. but he did a lot of other things, too	
_S_	4. once, he and his friends sailed to an island	
_F_	5. went there to find buried treasure	_subject_
_F_	6. didn't find any treasure	_subject_
_F_	7. Roosevelt something else, though	_verb_
_F_	8. found a nest with four baby birds in it	_subject_
_S_	9. he became an avid bird-watcher	

Fixing Fragments 2

The Next Step ● Go back to the fragments on page 53 and make them into complete sentences. Add a subject or a verb, whichever is needed. Use correct capitalization and punctuation.

(Answers may vary.)

1. **Franklin Roosevelt <u>was</u> president from 1933 to 1945.**

2. He was elected four times.

3. Mr. Roosevelt went there to find buried treasure.

4. He didn't find any treasure.

5. Roosevelt found something else, though.

6. He found a nest with four baby birds in it.

54 *Understanding Sentences*

Correcting Run-On Sentences 1

The First Step ● Your handbook explains a kind of sentence error called **run-on sentences**. (See page 87.) Here are two ways to correct run-on sentences: You can add end punctuation to split the run-on sentence into two sentences; or you can add punctuation and a connecting word to make one correct sentence.

DIRECTIONS: Correct the run-on sentences below by dividing them into two sentences. Use correct capitalization and end punctuation in your new sentences. If the sentence is not a run-on sentence, put a check mark next to it. The first sentence has been corrected for you.

_____ 1. Mark Twain wrote *Tom Sawyer* and *Huckleberry Finn*. He is one

of America's most famous authors.

_____ 2. He was born in Missouri. He traveled all over the world.

✓ 3. Before he became a writer, Twain was a riverboat pilot.

✓ 4. He worked on steamboats on the Mississippi River until the

Civil War started and the river was blockaded.

_____ 5. Twain was also a silver miner in Nevada. He was a

newspaper reporter, too.

✓ 6. Later, he lived in Hartford, Connecticut, with his wife and kids.

_____ 7. Mark Twain's real name was Samuel Clemens. Mark Twain was

a "pen name."

The Next Step ● Now correct all the run-on sentences above using a comma and a connecting word (*and, so, but, yet*). For example:
1. **Mark Twain wrote <u>Tom Sawyer</u> and <u>Huckleberry Finn</u>, and he is one of America's most famous authors.**

Correcting Run-On Sentences 2

The First Step ● In this activity, you'll practice correcting **run-on sentences** by adding a comma and a connecting word to make one correct sentence.

DIRECTIONS: Correct the run-on sentences below by adding a comma and a connecting word (*and, so, but, yet*). If the sentence is not a run-on sentence, put a check mark next to it. The first sentence has been corrected for you.

_____ 1. Anna Moses was a famous artist *, but* she didn't begin painting until she was 78 years old.

_____ 2. She enjoyed painting scenes near her farm in New York *, and* she often gave away her paintings.

_____ 3. One day an art collector saw her paintings in a store window *, and* he liked them very much.

__✓__ 4. He went to her home and bought every painting she had—15 of them!

_____ 5. Three of those paintings ended up in the Museum of Modern Art *, so* Anna Moses was a big success.

_____ 6. Her style of painting was called American Primitive *, yet* she became famous even in Europe.

__✓__ 7. She was known as Grandma Moses and lived to be 101.

The Next Step ● Which of the above run-on sentences could be corrected using a semicolon instead of a comma and a connecting word? See topic number 25 on page 347 in your handbook for more information on semicolons.

Correcting Rambling Sentences

The First Step ● Your handbook explains different kinds of sentence errors and how to correct them. (See handbook page 87.) This activity gives you practice correcting one kind of sentence error, **rambling sentences**.

DIRECTIONS: Below are two rambling sentences. Correct them by dividing them into as many sentences as you think are needed. Cross out the extra *and*'s, capitalize the first word of each sentence, and use the correct end punctuation. The first sentence has been done for you.

1. Our class went to the art museum. and a man who worked there gave us a special tour. and He told us about all the artists and when they lived. and He told us that one artist named Vincent van Gogh cut off his own ear! and Raul asked why. and our guide said that nobody knew for sure. and Raul thinks that van Gogh must have been nuts.

2. Maria's mom owns a restaurant called Old Mexico. and It's near our school. and Maria's mom invited our whole class to come to the restaurant for lunch. and Our teacher said that we could go. so we went today. and We all got to have anything we wanted. and almost everybody had two desserts. and It was great!

Correcting Rambling Sentences

The Next Step ● You and a classmate each write a rambling sentence. (See how long you can make it!) Then trade and correct each other's sentences.

Name

Subject-Verb Agreement 1

The First Step ● One basic rule of writing sentences is that the subject and verb must "agree." Sentence agreement is explained on page 88 in your handbook.

DIRECTIONS: Check the following sentences for subject-verb agreement. If the sentence is correct, put a check mark in front of it. If the subject and verb do not agree, correct the verb. An example has been done for you.

_____ 1. Americans speaks more than 100 different languages.

_____ 2. Many people moves to the United States from other countries.

✓ 3. They bring their languages with them.

_____ 4. Most immigrants comes from Mexico, Vietnam, and the Philippines.

_____ 5. My friend Annie speak Tagalog.

✓ 6. She is from the Philippines.

_____ 7. Jorge and Marta speaks Spanish.

✓ 8. English and Spanish are the most common languages in the United States.

_____ 9. Some native-born Americans speaks languages besides English.

_____ 10. For example, Native Americans *have* has their own languages.

✓ 11. My aunt is from Hawaii.

_____ 12. She know both Hawaiian and English.

© Great Source. All rights reserved.

Understanding Sentences **59**

Subject-Verb Agreement 2

The First Step ● Making subjects and verbs agree can be harder when the sentence has a compound subject. Review the material about compound subjects on page 88 in your handbook.

DIRECTIONS: In some of the following sentences, the subject and verb do not agree. Correct the verbs in those sentences. Put a check mark in front of the sentences that are correct. The first sentence has been done for you.

_____ 1. My mother or sisters asks/ me questions in Spanish.

_____ 2. Ricki and Rhoda takes/ me to the movies.

_____ 3. The teacher or the principal make the announcements. _(s ^)_

_____ 4. The first baseman or the shortstop bat first. _(s ^)_

__✓__ 5. My brothers and their dog go to the park.

_____ 6. Rick or his sisters takes/ the trash out.

_____ 7. My family and my school recycles/ paper.

__✓__ 8. My mom or my sisters drive me to school.

_____ 9. My sisters or my mom drive me to school. _(s ^)_

_____ 10. Several cars or a bus take us on field trips. _(s ^)_

The Next Step ● Using one of the sentences above as a starting point, write a short, funny story. Use as many compound subjects as you can, but be sure that your verbs always agree. Refer to page 88 in your handbook to check your writing. (Write your story on your own paper.)

Sentence Problems

The First Step ● Page 89 in your handbook explains four common kinds of **sentence problems**. Review them. Which ones sometimes creep into your sentences?

DIRECTIONS: Most of the following sentences contain sentence problems. Correct them by crossing out or changing the word that is incorrect. If the sentence is correct, make a check on the blank in front of it. The first sentence has been done for you.

_____ 1. People who move to the United States from other countries ~~they~~

are called immigrants.

_____ 2. If there had been no immigrants, there wouldn't be ~~nobody~~ *anybody* in the

United States except Native Americans.

✓ 3. The United States was once considered a melting pot, blending

many cultures into one.

_____ 4. My friend and her father arrived two years ago from India, and

they
~~he~~ will be happy to become U.S. citizens.

_____ 5. Some people say immigrants should ~~of~~ *have* stayed in the countries they

came from.

_____ 6. But that doesn't make ~~no~~ sense.

_____ 7. Most of us ~~we~~ are either immigrants or descendants of immigrants.

Sentence Problems

The Next Step ● Decide which kind of sentence problem is the biggest problem *for you*. Choose a partner, and ask your partner to write a few sentences that contain that sentence problem. Meanwhile, you write a few sentences that contain your partner's biggest sentence problem! Trade papers, and correct each other's sentences.

Combining Sentences 1

The First Step ● Pages 91 and 92 in your handbook explain ways to **combine sentences** using words and phrases. Review those pages; then do this practice activity.

DIRECTIONS: Combine the following pairs of sentences into one sentence using the methods on pages 91 and 92. The words in parentheses tell you which method to use. The first sentence has been done for you.

1. Pizza is cheesy. Pizza is gooey. Pizza is great. (series of words)

   Pizza is cheesy, gooey, and great.

2. Susan is tall. Susan is skinny. Susan is a fast runner. (series of words)

   Susan is tall, skinny, and a fast runner.

3. At camp we play baseball. We jump on a trampoline. (compound verb)

   At camp we play baseball and jump on a trampoline.

4. Marcia goes to the lake. She swims to the buoy and back. (compound verb)

   Marcia goes to the lake and swims to the buoy and back.

5. Sue won a golf tournament. She is my writing partner. (appositive phrase)

   Sue, my writing partner, won a golf tournament.

6. Todd got the Frisbee. He got it off the roof. (prepositional phrase)

   Todd got the Frisbee off the roof.

7. Karen got a new bike. It's a 12-speed. (key word)

   Karen got a new 12-speed bike.

Combining Sentences 2

The First Step ● One way to **combine sentences** is to make complex sentences. You connect two ideas with a subordinate conjunction. Your handbook explains complex sentences on page 93.

DIRECTIONS: Combine the following pairs of sentences to make complex sentences. Be sure to use a subordinate conjunction as explained in your handbook on page 387. The first one has been done for you.

(Answers will vary.)

1. Millions of Jewish people left Russia. They faced prejudice there.

   Millions of Jewish people left Russia because they faced prejudice

   there.

2. People from Great Britain found it easy to adjust to the United States. They already spoke English.

   People from Great Britain found it easy to adjust to the United

   States since they already spoke English.

3. Most Irish immigrants came during the 1800's. There was a famine in Ireland.

   Most Irish immigrants came during the 1800's when there was a

   famine in Ireland.

4. Many people from Sweden settled in Minnesota. They knew how to farm in cold weather.

   Many people from Sweden settled in Minnesota since they knew how

   to farm in cold weather.

The Next Step ● Write a complex sentence using a subordinate conjunction that you did not use in the sentences above.

Combining Sentences 3

The First Step ● One way to **combine sentences** is to make complex sentences. You may combine two ideas using a relative pronoun. Your handbook explains this on page 93. For more information about relative pronouns, see page 379.

DIRECTIONS: Combine the following pairs of sentences to make complex sentences. Use relative pronouns as explained in your handbook. The first one has been done for you.

1. Greek immigrants often opened restaurants in the United States. They had been farmers in Greece.

   Greek immigrants, who had been farmers in Greece, often opened

   restaurants in the United States.

2. Most Italian immigrants settled near other Italians. They had strong family ties.

   Most Italian immigrants, who had strong family ties, settled near

   other Italians.

3. The Vietnam War resulted in many Vietnamese people coming to the United States. The war ended in 1975.

   The Vietnam War, which ended in 1975, resulted in many Vietnamese

   people coming to the United States.

4. African-Americans make up about 12 percent of Americans. African-Americans' ancestors were often brought here as slaves.

   African-Americans, whose ancestors were often brought here as

   slaves, make up about 12 percent of Americans.

Combining Sentences 4

The First Step ● You've already had some practice **combining sentences**. You've seen how sentence combining can make your writing smoother and more interesting. Now review pages 90-93 in your handbook and get ready for a challenge!

DIRECTIONS: Rewrite the following paragraphs on the lines below. Combine short, choppy sentences to make smooth ones. Combine them however you choose, as long as the meaning stays the same and your sentences are correct.

There was a barn. It was dusty. It was made of wood. The wood was old. The wood was gray. The nails marked their age. They showed signs of permanent rust. There was an old silo. It stood next to the barn. It looked queer. It was every bit as old as the barn.

Just then, Penny appeared. She appeared in front of the barn. The animals looked up at her. They were surprised. Penny never came into the barnyard. Not at this time of day.

(Answers will vary.)

The Next Step ● Turn to page 154 in your handbook. Read the first two paragraphs of "Montgomery Mews Mysteriously." How do they compare to your paragraphs?

Making Compound Sentences

The First Step ● This workshop activity gives you practice combining sentences by making **compound sentences**. See page 93 of your handbook for information about compound sentences.

DIRECTIONS: Combine the following pairs of sentences into one compound sentence. Remember, use a comma and words such as *and, but, so,* or *for* to make compound sentences. The first sentence has been done for you.

1. I know three kids from other countries. I like them.

   I know three kids from other countries, and I like them.

2. Two of them are from Mexico. One is from India.

   Two of them are from Mexico, and one is from India.

3. They have different holidays. It's interesting to learn about them.

   They have different holidays, and it's interesting to learn about

   them.

4. In Mexico, they have Cinco de Mayo. In India, they have Divali.

   In Mexico, they have Cinco de Mayo, and in India, they have Divali.

5. I don't speak Spanish or Marathi. My friends speak English.

   I don't speak Spanish or Marathi, but my friends speak English.

Making Compound Sentences

The Next Step ● Write a paragraph or short story about a holiday or custom your family observes. After you've finished, go back and check your sentences. Should any of your short sentences be combined into compound sentences? If so, change them before you exchange your stories.

_____

_____

_____

_____

_____

_____

_____

_____

_____

_____

_____

_____

_____

_____

Name _____

Types of Sentences 1

The First Step ● Read about **simple**, **compound**, and **complex** **sentences** on page 373 in your handbook. If you're not sure you understand how to tell the three types of sentences apart, turn to pages 91-93. All the model sentences on pages 91-92 are simple sentences. Compound and complex sentences are modeled on page 93.

DIRECTIONS: Here is part of the model book review of *The True Confessions of Charlotte Doyle* on page 133 in your handbook. On the lines below, write *simple, compound,* or *complex* to identify each sentence. The hardest sentence has been done for you!

1. The True Confessions of Charlotte Doyle is about a wealthy thirteen-year-old girl named Charlotte.   *simple*

2. In 1832, Charlotte is supposed to sail from England to Rhode Island with two other families, but the families never show up.   *compound*

3. Charlotte decides to sail with the crew alone.   *simple*

4. She becomes good friends with the captain, until the captain kills two of the crewmen for being traitors.   *complex*

5. Charlotte then decides to join the crew and becomes "Mr. Doyle" in the logbook.   *simple*

6. During a storm, the first mate, Hollybrass, is killed with her knife!   *simple*

7. I think Avi, the author, wanted to tell his readers that even people like Charlotte who are very shy can become strong and brave.   **complex**

8. She had to make many hard choices.   *simple*

9. I think he also wanted readers to understand that accusations aren't always true.   *complex*

10. I liked the book because Avi made all the characters seem real.   *complex*

Types of Sentences 2

The First Step ● Review the **types of sentences** on page 373 in your handbook before doing this practice activity. You may also want to read about clauses on page 372 and review the information about compound and complex sentences on page 93.

DIRECTIONS: Rewrite each of the following simple sentences twice. First add an independent clause (that is, another simple sentence) to make a compound sentence. Then add a dependent clause to make a complex sentence. An example has been done for you.

(Answers will vary.)

1. My brother has a new set of skates.

   compound: **My brother has a new set of skates, and he uses them every day.**

   complex: **My brother has a new set of skates that he uses every day.**

2. Her school has a computer club.

   compound: *Her school has a computer club, but she is not a member.*

   complex: *Her school has a computer club that has seven members.*

3. My dad cooks Italian food.

   compound: *My dad cooks Italian food, and it tastes great.*

   complex: *My dad cooks Italian food because he's Italian.*

4. Our teacher travels every summer.

   compound: *Our teacher travels every summer, and she brings back pictures.*

   complex: *Our teacher travels every summer after she runs the marathon.*

Simple and Compound Sentences

The First Step ● Recall as much as possible about **simple** and **compound sentences**. Then turn to page 373 in your handbook and carefully reread the section on simple and compound sentences.

Examples:

Simple Sentences

My sisters wanted to earn money for camp.
They decided to wash cars for $3.00 each.

Compound Sentence

My sisters wanted to earn money for camp,
so they decided to wash cars for $3.00 each.

DIRECTIONS: Think of a time you did something to earn money. Write four simple sentences about your experience. Then combine the sentences so you have two compound sentences. Check the coordinate conjunctions on page 387, and try to use a different one for each sentence. (See page 93 for more on compound sentences.)

Simple Sentences

1. _____ *(Answers will vary.)* _____

2. _____

3. _____

4. _____

Compound Sentences

1. _____ *(Answers will vary.)* _____

_____

2. _____

_____

The Next Step ● Check your compound sentences for proper punctuation. Did you use a comma before a conjunction? Or did you simply use a semicolon? What about end punctuation?

Kinds of Sentences

The First Step ● There are four kinds of sentences: **declarative**, **interrogative**, **imperative**, and **exclamatory**. Turn to page 373 in your handbook, and read the section about the four kinds of sentences.

Examples:

Declarative
The John Hancock Building and the Empire State Building are famous skyscrapers.

Interrogative
How many states can you see from the top of these buildings?

Imperative
You must go to the top.

Exclamatory
The people look like ants!

DIRECTIONS: Recall a time you had an awesome experience. Maybe you went to the top of a skyscraper, got stuck on the top of a Ferris wheel, or rode a dirt bike for the first time. Write one sentence of each kind about your experience.

Declarative _____ *(Answers will vary.)* _____

_____

Interrogative _____

_____

Imperative _____

_____

Exclamatory _____

_____

Parts of Speech Review

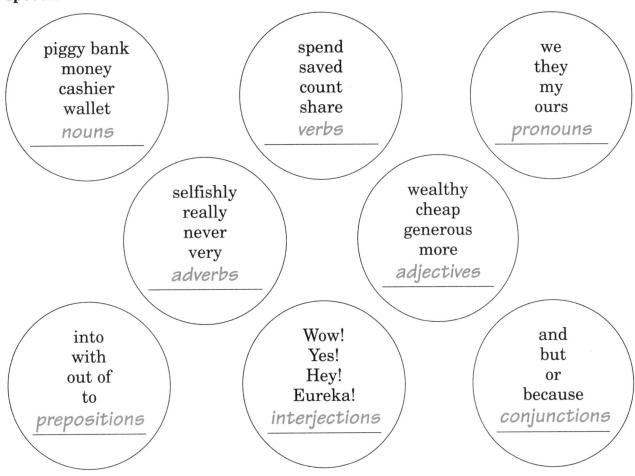

The First Step ● Each of the **eight parts of speech** is important, but some words are more meaningful than others. We think that nouns carry the most meaning. See what you think when you finish this page.

DIRECTIONS: Identify the part of speech for each list of words by writing it on the line in the circle. See page 374 in your handbook for a list of the eight parts of speech.

piggy bank
money
cashier
wallet
nouns

spend
saved
count
share
verbs

we
they
my
ours
pronouns

selfishly
really
never
very
adverbs

wealthy
cheap
generous
more
adjectives

into
with
out of
to
prepositions

Wow!
Yes!
Hey!
Eureka!
interjections

and
but
or
because
conjunctions

The Next Step ● Now write a sentence using as many of the parts of speech as you can. You may want to use some of the words in the circles.

_____

_____

_____

Identifying Common and Proper Nouns

> **The First Step** ● Nouns can be labeled as **common** or **proper**. Check your handbook if you need an explanation of these terms. (See handbook page 375.)

DIRECTIONS: Underline each noun in the sentences below; then write **C** above each common noun and **P** above each proper noun. (The number of nouns in each sentence has been given in parentheses.)

　　　　P　　　　　　　C　　　　　P　　　　　　　　　　C　　　　　　　C
　　Juan bought a bike from Green's, a hardware store in his neighborhood.

　　　　　　　　　　　　　　　　　　　　C
(5) He bought a secondhand Schwinn bike, and it seemed to be in very good

　　C　　　　　　　　　　　　　　C　　　　P　　　　　　　　　　P
condition. (2) He bought the bike on Saturday, rode it around on Sunday, but

　　　P　　　　　　C　　　　　　　　　　　　　　　　　　P
on Monday the handlebars started wobbling. (5) On Tuesday, he took his

　　　　　C　　　　　　　　C　　　　　　　P　　　　　C
Schwinn bike back to the store and told Mr. Green, the owner, about the

　　C　　　　　　P　　　　　　　　　　　C　　　　　　　C
handlebars. (6) Mr. Green got out his wrench and a couple bolts and fixed the

　　C　　　　　　　　　　　P　　　　　　　　　　　　　　　　　C
handlebars right away! (4) Now Juan thinks his secondhand bike is better

　　　　　　　　　　C　　　P
than all the new bikes at Green's. (4)

> **The Next Step** ● Look around you and notice all the persons, places, things, and ideas. Then make two lists—one of proper nouns and one of common nouns. See how many you can spot!
>
> | Proper Nouns | Common Nouns |
> |---|---|
> | | |

Uses of Nouns

The First Step ● Nouns can be used in different ways in sentences. You've had lots of practice using **subject nouns**, which are nouns used as the subject of a sentence. But you also need to know how to use **predicate nouns** and **possessive nouns**. Read about all three uses on page 376 in your handbook.

DIRECTIONS: In the sentences below, label all the underlined nouns. Write an **S** above the noun if it is a subject noun, a **P** if it is a predicate noun, and a **POS** if it is a possessive noun. The first sentence has been done for you.

1. A (S) beagle is a friendly (P) dog.

2. The (S) party will be a (P) surprise.

3. (POS) Jeremy's (S) cat is a (P) Siamese.

4. (POS) Marla's favorite (S) sport is (P) baseball.

5. (S) Jordan became an (P) artist.

6. The (S) winner was (P) Suzanne.

7. (S) Blake knows (POS) Lydia's brother.

8. The (POS) book's (S) author signed my copy.

9. Our (POS) school's (S) track team won the championship.

10. My best hiding (S) place is the (P) attic.

The Next Step ● Fill in each blank below with a predicate noun.

1. The laziest color is _____ .

2. My worst day is _____.

3. The best sport is _____ .

4. My favorite animal is the _____ .

Nouns As Objects

The First Step ● A noun is a **direct object** when it receives the action of the verb. A noun is an **indirect object** when it names the person to or for whom something is done. A noun is an **object of a preposition** when it is part of a prepositional phrase.

DIRECTIONS: Look at the following sentences and the circled nouns in each. Then label each noun according to which kind of object it is. (Use page 376 in your handbook as a guide.)

Yelena wrote a funny (letter.) _____*direct object*_____

Yelena wrote (Mike) a funny letter. _____*indirect object*_____

Yelena wrote a funny letter to (Mike.) ___*object of a preposition*___

DIRECTIONS: Now write three sentences on your own. Each one should contain a noun used as a different kind of object. Your sentences may contain more than one kind of object. *Special Challenge:* You may want to write with compound objects just the way you write with compound subjects. Check out this example:

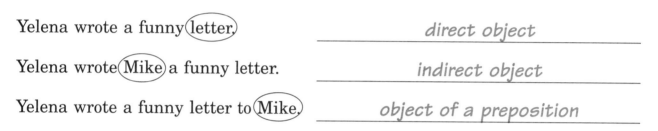

(direct object)
Yelena wrote a funny **letter** to **Mike** and **Maggie**.
(compound object of a preposition)

1. _____*(Answers will vary.)*_____

_____

2. _____

_____

3. _____

_____

The Next Step ● When you're finished, exchange your work with a classmate. Find and label the nouns used as objects. Did your partner write at least one example of each?

Pronouns

The First Step ● Read about "Person of a Pronoun" on page 378 in your handbook. The **person of a pronoun** indicates the point of view of a story. The activities below will help you explore different points of view.

Examples from *Cinderella*:

First-Person Point of View

    I cleaned and scrubbed the cottage all day.

Second-Person Point of View

    You two will go to the ball to meet the prince.

Third-Person Point of View

    She had to leave the ball by midnight.

DIRECTIONS: Write a different ending to *Cinderella*. Write it from the first-person or third-person point of view. Circle five pronouns in your story. Are most of them in the same person?

(Answers will vary.)

_____

_____

_____

_____

_____

_____

_____

The Next Step ● In a small group, share your story endings and decide which point of view was used in each of them.

Person of a Pronoun

The First Step ● Review the lists of personal pronouns in your handbook (page 377), and also the section on **Person of a Pronoun** (page 378).

DIRECTIONS: In the following sentences, underline the personal pronouns. Above each pronoun, write a 1, 2, or 3 to show whether it is a first-person pronoun, second-person pronoun, or third-person pronoun. The first two sentences have been done for you.

1. ③She likes ①me, and ①I like ③her.

2. Do ②you want to play volleyball with ①us?

3. ①I made lemonade, and ③they built a sand castle.

4. ③They built a moat around ③it.

5. Where did ②you and ③he go?

6. Do ②you and ③she want to come with ①me?

7. ②You should ride ③his bike.

8. ③They don't know where ③her car is.

9. ③He borrowed a bike from ③her because ③she wasn't going to use ③it.

10. ②You can return ③it to ①us or to ③them.

11. Is ①my bike in ②your car or in ③their car?

Types of Verbs

The First Step ● Review **Types of Verbs** on page 380 in your handbook before you do this activity.

DIRECTIONS: Read the following sentences and look at the underlined verbs. Decide whether the verbs are action verbs **(A)**, linking verbs **(L)**, or helping verbs **(H)**. Write the correct letter above each. The first one has been done for you.

1. Rolf, our bulldog, <u>loves</u> doggy biscuits.
   (A)

2. Those biscuits must <u>taste</u> good, because he <u>hides</u> them everywhere.
   (L) ... *(A)*

3. Then he <u>can</u> <u>snack</u> anytime.
   (H) *(A)*

4. I <u>have</u> <u>found</u> biscuits in my shoes.
   (H) *(A)*

5. Dad <u>has</u> <u>spotted</u> biscuits under his chewed-up gloves.
   (H) *(A)*

6. Rolf <u>chews</u> gloves, too . . . and socks.
   (A)

7. Oh, yes, and Rolf <u>sneaks</u> cookies, but only the fresh-baked kind.
   (A)

8. Our family <u>has</u> <u>grown</u> fond of Rolf, though.
   (H) *(L)*

9. At least he <u>smells</u> sweet.
   (L)

10. Rolf always <u>spills</u> my bath powder on his way through the bathroom.
    (A)

Types of Verbs

The Next Step ● Pretend that you have a new pen pal.
Write a letter in which you introduce yourself; tell about your
life, family, and friends; and ask your pen pal about his or her
life.   After you finish, go back and underline all the verbs in
your letter, and label each one as an action verb (A), a
linking verb (L), or a helping verb (H).

_____

_____

_____

_____

_____

_____

_____

_____

_____

_____

_____

_____

_____

Using Irregular Verbs

The First Step ● **Irregular verbs** don't play by the rules! When you make them past tense, you can't just add "ed" as you do with regular verbs. The only way to learn the past tense and past participles of irregular verbs is to memorize each one. And that takes practice.

DIRECTIONS: Study the chart of irregular verbs on page 382 in your handbook. Then close your handbook and fill in the missing words in the chart below.

present tense	past tense	past participle
1. blow	blew	**blown**
2. bring	brought	**brought**
3. draw	drew	drawn
4. eat	**ate**	eaten
5. fly	flew	flown
6. hang	hung	**hung**
7. hide	**hid**	hidden
8. know	knew	known
9. lay (to put in place)	laid	laid
10. lie (to lie down)	**lay**	lain
11. run	ran	**run**
12. see	**saw**	seen

The Next Step ● Now check your work. Turn to the chart on page 382 and look up each word you filled in. Make a list of all the verbs you got wrong, and write sentences using each one. (If you didn't make any mistakes, choose any two verbs and write sentences using them.)

Irregular Verbs

The First Step ● **Irregular verbs** are not normal! When you change them to past tense or use them with a helping verb, they change in different ways. The only way to know how they change is to learn the different forms of each verb.

DIRECTIONS: Fill in the chart below to see how well you know the different forms for nine common irregular verbs. The first one has been done for you.

Present Tense	Past Tense	Past Participle
see	*saw*	seen
write	wrote	*written*
drive	*drove*	*driven*
freeze	*froze*	frozen
burst	burst	*burst*
begin	*began*	*begun*
blow	blew	blown
give	gave	*given*
speak	*spoke*	*spoken*

The Next Step ● Now check your work. Turn to the chart on page 382 and look up each word you filled in. Make a list of all the verbs you got wrong, and write a sentence using each one.

The Tense of a Verb

The First Step ● The **present tense** of a verb states an action that is happening now, or that happens regularly. The **past tense** of a verb states an action that happened at a specific time in the past. The **future tense** of a verb states an action that will take place. (See handbook page 383.)

Examples:

Present Tense   The cricket, mouse, and cat **enjoy** talking to each other.

Past Tense   They **pranced** about the newsstand half the night.

Future Tense   The three characters **will win** the hearts of their readers.

DIRECTIONS: These three sentences are about the gentle animals in *Cricket in Times Square* by George Sheldon. Now *you* write some sentences about imaginary animals that you have read about or seen in a cartoon. Write at least two sentences for each of the tenses.

Present Tense Sentences: _____ (Answers will vary.) _____

_____

_____

_____

Past Tense Sentences: _____

_____

_____

_____

Future Tense Sentences: _____

_____

_____

_____

The Tense of a Verb

The Next Step ● Write a paragraph about the way you think something will be in the future (cars, schools, television). Write your paragraph in the future tense. Share your writing with a classmate. Make sure that each sentence is written in the future tense.

Adjectives

The First Step ● An **adjective** is a word that describes a noun or a pronoun. Adjectives are used in both the subject and predicate part of the sentence. (See handbook page 384.)

DIRECTIONS: Write four adjectives to describe each of the different moods pictured below.

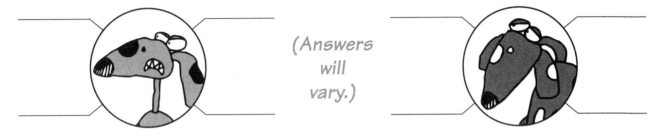

(Answers will vary.)

The Next Step ● Let's say the dog's name is Chester. Write an acrostic poem, using adjectives to describe him. You may use some of the adjectives above, and you may need to think of some new ones.

C _____ (Answers will vary.) _____

H _____

E _____

S _____

T _____

E _____

R _____

All About Adjectives and You

The First Step ● Turn to page 384 in your handbook and read about the **comparative** and **superlative** forms of adjectives. Also check the "Special Forms" section on that page.

Examples of some special forms of adjectives:

Sam is the **best** keyboard player in the class.

He is even **better** than his teacher.

He knows **more** songs by heart than anyone else.

DIRECTIONS: Write about something that you can do very well. (This is a chance to boast about yourself a little!) Use as many comparative and superlative forms of adjectives as possible. Underline your adjectives.

(Answers will vary.)

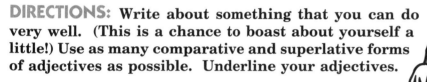

The Next Step ● Share your writing with a partner. After you've read about each other's talents, label all the comparative and superlative adjectives.

Name _____

All About Adverbs

The First Step ● Most **adverbs** tell where, how, or when. They describe a verb, an adjective, or another adverb. See page 385 in your handbook for more about adverbs.

DIRECTIONS: In each of the following sentences, circle the adverb and draw a line to the word it describes. On the line next to the sentence, write whether the adverb tells where, how, or when. The first two sentences have been done for you.

1. Jody and I (often) go to the park.   *when*

2. (Sometimes) we play softball.   *when*

3. We choose our teams (carefully.)   *how*

4. We play (hard) and play to win.   *how*

5. Jody and I (always) pitch.   *when*

6. Tasha (never) strikes out.   *when*

7. Ira hits the ball (hard.)   *how*

8. Most fielders step (back) for Ira.   *where*

9. Monica (easily) catches ground balls.   *how*

DIRECTIONS: In each of the following sentences, add an adverb that answers the question in parentheses. Write the new sentence on the line. Then, circle the adverb and draw a line to the word it describes. The first one has been done for you.

I'm going to the park. (when)   *I'm going to the park (later.)*

Marcia eats. (how)   *(Answers will vary.)*

Rodrigo laughs. (how) _____

Let's go swimming. (when) _____

© Great Source. All rights reserved.

Understanding Our Language **87**

All About Adverbs

_____

_____

_____

_____

_____

_____

_____

_____

_____

_____

_____

_____

_____

_____

_____

Forms of Adverbs

The First Step ● Review page 385 in your handbook. Then do this activity to practice using the different forms of **adverbs**.

DIRECTIONS: Rewrite each sentence below two times. In your first sentence, use the comparative form of the underlined adverb. In your second sentence, use the superlative form of the same adverb. An example has been done for you.

(Answers will vary.)

1. Gabriella runs <u>fast</u>.

   Bev runs faster than Sarah.

   Teri runs fastest of all.

2. Bruce played <u>well</u>.

   played better

   played best

3. Larissa plays her CD's <u>loudly</u>.

   more loudly

   most loudly

4. Terrence reads <u>slowly</u>.

   more slowly

   most slowly

5. Spot panted <u>eagerly</u>.

   more eagerly

   most eagerly

Forms of Adverbs

The Next Step ● Think of three adverbs that describe *how* something is done. Then write sentences using the positive, comparative, and superlative forms of each adverb. A sample has been done for you.

1. adverb = *carefully*

   Jim writes his stories carefully.

   Rosa writes hers more carefully than Jim.

   Clare writes hers most carefully of all.

2. adverb =

3. adverb =

4. adverb =

Prepositions

> **The First Step** ● Turn to page 386 in your handbook and review the information about **prepositional phrases**.

Examples:

> I went **to a concert** this summer.
>
> I sat **in the first row.**

DIRECTIONS: Pretend that you really did go to a concert. Write a friendly letter telling one of your best friends about it. Describe what you did. Put parentheses around the prepositional phrases you use in your letter.

M·m·m·m·m·

Dear _____,

_____

_____

(Answers will vary.)

_____

_____

_____

> **The Next Step** ● Try reading your letter and leaving out all of the prepositional phrases. What happens?

Your friend,

_____

Name

Interjections

The First Step ● An **interjection** is a word or phrase used to express strong emotions or surprise. A comma or an exclamation point is used to separate an interjection from the rest of the sentence. (See page 387 in your handbook.)

Examples:

Wow! Does it bite?

Hey! I think you better hold him now!

Man! I wouldn't do that!

Yikes! Let her have the first turn!

DIRECTIONS: Pretend you just spent some time with a herpetologist (someone who works with snakes and other reptiles). Write a postcard telling a friend how you felt about being around snakes. Did you hold the snake, or did you just watch? Use interjections to let your friend know how strongly you felt about this experience.

_____, 199__

Dear _____, ___

_____

_____

(Answers will vary.)

_____

From,

_____

Using Conjunctions

The First Step ● **Conjunctions** are words that connect words, phrases, or clauses. Your handbook explains conjunctions on page 387. In this activity, you'll practice using all three kinds of conjunctions: coordinate conjunctions, subordinate conjunctions, and correlative conjunctions.

DIRECTIONS: Connect each group of words below to make one sentence, using a conjunction. Check your handbook to first decide which of the three kinds of conjunctions to use. Then choose the best conjunction. A few examples have been done for you.

(Answers will vary.)

1. Marci brought cake to class. Marci brought ice cream to class.

    Marci brought cake and ice cream to class. (coordinate)

2. Jason got the flu. He played football in the rain.

    Jason got the flu after he played football in the rain. (subordinate)

3. Our teacher may lead the assembly. Our principal may lead the assembly.

    Either our teacher or our principal may lead the assembly. (correlative)

4. Yelena got a new haircut. She doesn't like it.

    Yelena got a new haircut, but she doesn't like it. (coordinate)

5. Josh wanted to come. He had a cold.

    Josh wanted to come, but he had a cold. (coordinate)

6. My dog got sick. He ate a whole box of cookies.

    My dog got sick because he ate a whole box of cookies. (subordinate)

Coordinate Conjunctions

> **The First Step** ● **Coordinate conjunctions** connect equal parts. For example, coordinate conjunctions can connect two words, two phrases, or two clauses. (See page 387 in your handbook.)

DIRECTIONS: Use one of the coordinate conjunctions listed in the box to fill in the blank in each sentence below.

and	but	or	so	yet

1. My dog Harold is small _____ *but* _____ strong.

2. He has white paws _____ *and* _____ shaggy ears.

3. All afternoon he sleeps on the porch _____ *or* _____ in the house.

4. When I get home, he wants to run _____ *and* _____ play.

5. Harold is fat _____ *yet* _____ fast.

DIRECTIONS: Coordinate conjunctions can be used to connect two simple sentences and make a compound sentence. (Pages 86 and 373 in your handbook explain compound sentences.) Use a comma, plus a coordinate conjunction from the box above, to connect each pair of simple sentences below.

(Answers will vary.)

1. Harold loves dog food. He loves people food, too.

   Harold loves dog food, but he loves people food, too.

2. I give Harold cookies. He's always happy to see me.

   I give Harold cookies, so he's always happy to see me.

3. He likes hamburgers. He's not supposed to have them.

   He likes hamburgers, yet he's not supposed to have them.

4. Harold loves bones. He looks for them in grocery bags.

   Harold loves bones, and he looks for them in grocery bags.

Subordinate Conjunctions

The First Step ● Use a **subordinate conjunction** to connect two clauses to make a complex sentence. (See page 387 in your handbook.)

DIRECTIONS: Choose subordinate conjunctions from the list in the box below and write them on the lines to complete the story.

> **after, although, as if, because, before, if, in order that, since, so, that, though, unless, until, when, where, while**

We were in art class _____*when*_____ our principal reminded

everyone that the dress rehearsal before the concert would begin at 6:00 p.m.,

sharp! _____*Because*_____ Matt arrived just five minutes before the concert,

Mr. Martin, the choir director, told him that he would have to miss out on the

party. _____*After*_____ the concert was over, Matt raced off the bleachers

and disappeared. We spotted him using the office phone. We were surprised

to see Matt at the party later _____*until*_____ he explained his reason for

being late. Matt's new brother had just been born!

Subordinate Conjunctions

The Next Step ● Now write your own school-related story. Use a variety of subordinate conjunctions to make at least three complex sentences. *Hint:* You may begin a complex sentence with a subordinate conjunction.

_____

_____

_____

_____

_____

_____

_____

_____

_____

_____

_____

_____

_____

_____

_____

Minilessons

The minilessons in this section cover basic editing and proofreading skills. All the minilessons are cross-referenced with the handbook.

Marking Punctuation Minilessons

Double Up . . . .*Using Semicolons*

READ about semicolons on **page 347** in your handbook. Then WRITE three compound sentences, using semicolons to COMBINE the simple sentences (also called independent clauses) below.

> I'm going to the zoo tomorrow.
> That's the best place to see the fireworks.
> The reptile house is what I want to see.
> I'll have chocolate chip.
> The ice-cream truck has lots of flavors.
> We're going to the city park on the Fourth of July.

1. *I'm going to the zoo tomorrow; the reptile house is what I want to see.*

2. *We're going to the city park on the Fourth of July; that's the best place to see the fireworks.*

3. *The ice-cream truck has lots of flavors; I'll have chocolate chip.*

Next WRITE two simple sentences of your own.

1. _____*(Answers will vary.)*_____

2. _____

Then USE a semicolon to combine your two simple sentences into one sentence.

1. _____

_____

A Worm-Digging Experience .... *Hyphens*

FILL IN the blanks with hyphenated adjectives formed from the list of words below. See handbook **page 348** for help. The first one has been done for you.

1. My _____ **worm-digging** _____ brother makes big bucks selling bait!

2. That _____ *mouse-loving* _____ cat brings its prey home. Yuck!

3. The plate held my _____ *half-eaten* _____ lunch.

4. Take a picture of those _____ *tree-covered* _____ mountains.

5. The _____ *heart-pounding* _____ mystery story kept me awake.

> digging   half   loving   pounding   covered
>
> mouse   worm   tree   eaten   heart

I told her not to—BANG!—slam the door. .... *Dashes*

To each of the following sentences, ADD a word or phrase that needs to be set off with a dash. Remember, dashes set off a quick change in direction, or an interruption in the flow of thought. An example has been done for you. (See **page 348** in your handbook.)

(Answers will vary.)

1. The baseball landed right in the potato salad.

The baseball landed—plop!—right in the potato salad.

2. The dog barked and ran out the door.

The dog barked—bowwow—and ran out the door.

3. I finally finished my chores and went swimming.

I finally finished my chores—whew!—and went swimming.

4. I cut my hand on the sharp metal can.

I cut my hand—ouch—on the sharp metal can.

5. She went to Jody's. She went to Angie's.

She went to Jody's—no—to Angie's.

Shorten it! . . . . *Contractions*

MAKE CONTRACTIONS from the following phrases. If you need help, check **page 349** in your handbook. To check your work, look up your contractions in a dictionary.

1. I will   *I'll*

2. could not   *couldn't*

3. have not   *haven't*

4. she would   *she'd*

5. does not   *doesn't*

6. They are   *They're*

7. it is   *it's*

8. Let us   *Let's*

9. cannot   *can't*

10. should have   *should've*

Charlie's Horse . . . . *Possessives*

LIST the names of seven people you know. Next to each name, WRITE its possessive form. (*Hint:* You'll need seven apostrophes. See your handbook, **page 349**, topic number 45, for details!)

1. *(Answers will vary.)*

2.

3.

4.

5.

6.

7.

To each of the following sentences, ADD a word or phrase that needs to be set off with parentheses. Remember, parentheses set off words that add information or make something clearer. An example has been done for you. Also see **page 351** in your handbook.

(Answers will vary.)

1. My sisters gang up on me.

   My sisters (they're twins) gang up on me.

2. My cousin is in the air force.

   My cousin (she flew her first plane at age 15) is in the air force.

3. My aunt plays in an orchestra.

   My aunt (who always sends me savings bonds for my birthday) plays in an orchestra.

4. We wanted to play outdoors, but the weather was bad.

   We wanted to play outdoors (behind the garage in the alley), but the weather was bad.

5. We didn't have enough people for a team.

   We didn't have enough people (eight players are too few) for a team.

Editing for Mechanics Minilessons

Name that place. . . . . *Capitalization*

Open your handbook to **page 353**, topic number 67. For each type of
geographic name listed, LIST two more examples. Do as many as you can
on your own; then check a map or an atlas if you need to.
SHARE your work.

(Answers will vary.)

1. Planets and heavenly bodies _____ _____

2. Continents _____ _____

3. Countries _____ _____

4. States _____ _____

5. Provinces _____ _____

6. Cities and counties _____ _____

7. Bodies of water _____ _____

8. Landforms _____ _____

9. Public areas _____ _____

10. Roads and highways _____ _____

11. Buildings _____ _____

To Cap or Not to Cap . . . . *Capitalization*

The following words are sometimes capitalized. It depends on how the word is
used in the sentence. (See handbook **pages 352-354**.)
WRITE two sentences using each word: one sentence in which the word is
capitalized, and one in which it is not. (*One more thing:* Do not use the
words as first words in your sentences!)

mother	north	white house
president	earth	war

Puppies on the Loose . . . . *Plurals*

IMAGINE that your dog has six puppies. One day while you're at school, the puppies romp through the house, destroying everything in sight.

WRITE a short story about the puppies' day, using the plural forms of as many of the following words as you can. (See handbook **page 355**.)

shoe *shoes*	dish *dishes*	tomato *tomatoes*	guppy *guppies*
sofa *sofas*	box *boxes*	turkey *turkeys*	paw *paws*
pillow *pillows*	candy *candies*	loaf *loaves*	nose *nose*

Zip Zap . . . . *Abbreviations*

See **page 146** of your handbook for help in changing the addresses below into the form preferred by the United States Postal Service. See **page 357** for abbreviations of the underlined words.

MS MAURA ANTHONY	*MS MAURA ANTHONY*
2635 <u>NORTH</u> PINE <u>STREET</u>	*2635 N PINE ST*
AUGUSTA <u>MAINE</u> 10000	*AUGUSTA ME 10000*
MR FELIX UNGER	*MR FELIX UNGER*
PRESIDENT	*PRESIDENT*
FOOTBALL FANS OF AMERICA	*FOOTBALL FANS OF AMERICA*
BOX 42	*BOX 42*
BUFFALO <u>NEW YORK</u> 14213	*BUFFALO NY 14213*

Then WRITE your name and address and the address of a friend or relative in the same form.

Don't MTB; it's PN! . . . . *Initialisms*

THINK of at least five phrases that you use all the time—"no way," "pizza night," "home before dark," "miss the bus," etc.

TURN all your phrases into initialisms. (Into what? Check your handbook, **page 356**, topic number 91.)

For Example: "miss the bus" becomes MTB; "pizza night" becomes PN.

Now WRITE a paragraph using all your initialisms.

TRADE paragraphs with a partner.

FIGURE OUT each other's initialisms. What do they stand for?

Checking Your Spelling Minilessons

Short, but Not Always Simple . . . . *Check Your Spelling*

Just because a word is short does not mean it is easy to spell. There may be a
   letter that you do not hear when you pronounce the word, or a sound that
   could be spelled several different ways.
LOOK for 10 three- or four-letter words in the list of commonly misspelled
   words on **pages 358-361** in your handbook. CHOOSE ones that cause you
   trouble, and write them down.
TALK about why each one might be easy to misspell.
WRITE a brief paragraph that uses as many of these short words as possible.
   UNDERLINE each short word that you used from your list.
ASK a partner to read your paragraph and check the spellings of your
   underlined words, using the list of commonly misspelled words.

Just add "ly." . . . . *Check Your Spelling*

Just by adding "ly" to many adjectives, you can change them into adverbs.
   See **pages 384-385** in your handbook for more information on adjectives
   and adverbs.
LIST all of the adverbs (formed by adding "ly" to an adjective) that you find in
   the list of commonly misspelled words on **pages 358-361** in your handbook.

(*Note:* Which word drops a final "e" before adding "ly"? _____*truly*_____)

1.	*exactly*	6.	*quickly*
2.	*finally*	7.	*really*
3.	*generally*	8.	*suddenly*
4.	*immediately*	9.	*unfortunately*
5.	*likely*	10.	*usually*

FIND four words in the list that you could change from adjectives to adverbs
   just by adding "ly."

11.	*(Answers will vary.)*	13.	*deliciously*
12.	*anonymously*	14.	*innocently*

Using the Right Word Minilessons

Captain, may I . . . . *Usage: "Can" or "May"?*

REWRITE each of the following sentences, using *can* or *may* (or *cannot* or *may not*) to REPLACE the underlined words. (See handbook **page 363**.)

1. I <u>am not able to</u> juggle four bananas at one time.

   I cannot juggle four bananas at one time.

2. I <u>am not allowed to</u> juggle bananas in the living room.

   I may not juggle bananas in the living room.

3. My dog <u>knows how to</u> fetch.

   My dog can fetch.

4. He also knows that he <u>is not allowed to</u> go into the living room.

   He also knows that he may not go into the living room.

5. My mother said I <u>am free to</u> go to the movies.

   My mother said I may go to the movies.

6. But I don't think I <u>will be able to</u> stay up that late.

   But I don't think I can stay up that late.

7. My dog <u>doesn't know how to</u> read or write.

   My dog cannot read or write.

8. But he still <u>gets to</u> go to school on Pet Day.

   But he still may go to school on Pet Day.

Flash the Fish . . . . *Usage: "Its" or "It's"?*

FILL IN the blanks in the sentences below, using "its" or "it's," whichever is correct. Check **page 365** of your handbook for help.

1. _____It's_____ time to give the goldfish _____its_____ food.

2. _____Its_____ name is Flash, and _____it's_____ a small goldfish.

3. It swims around in _____its_____ bowl, waiting for _____its_____ dinner.

4. _____It's_____ too bad Flash can't go anywhere.

5. But _____it's_____ safer for a goldfish to stay in _____its_____ bowl.

6. When you're a goldfish, _____it's_____ a big, dry world out there.

Who's on first? . . . . *Usage: "Whose" or "Who's"?*

FILL IN the blanks in the sentences below, using "whose" or "who's," whichever is correct. Check **page 369** of your handbook for help.

1. _____Whose_____ book is this?

2. It belongs to Jordan, _____who's_____ in my math class.

3. _____Who's_____ going to the recycling center?

4. _____Whose_____ turn is it to go?

5. This is Sanjeev, _____whose_____ family is from India.

6. Is he the one _____who's_____ new here?

7. _____Whose_____ science class are you in?

8. My teacher is Ms. Chang, _____who's_____ from China.

Understanding Sentences Minilessons

Then I heard . . . . *Kinds of Sentences*

IMAGINE yourself at a beach or pool in the summertime. People are swimming, diving, splashing, wading, talking, yelling, and laughing.

WRITE down at least eight sentences that you might overhear. Then READ each sentence and IDENTIFY the kinds of sentences you have written. (The four kinds of sentences are declarative, interrogative, imperative, and exclamatory.) Is one kind of sentence more common than another?

SHARE your work with another student.

Patchwork Stories . . . . *Sentence Fragments*

MAKE UP five sentence fragments. (See **page 87** in your handbook for an explanation of fragments.) Imagine that you will use them to write a story—make them as colorful and interesting as you can. Make sure some of the fragments need a subject, and some need a verb.

TRADE with a partner who has done the same thing. Turn each other's fragments into sentences that make a story. Your sentences can be funny or weird—as long as they're correct!

Says who? . . . . *Sentence Fragments*

Although sentence fragments are errors in your writing (see your handbook, **page 87**), they're okay in your talking! People use fragments all the time when they talk to each other:

"Going to the mall?"

"No money."

"Basketball?"

"Too cold."

WRITE a short conversation between two people. Make everything they say a fragment.

Then REWRITE each piece of dialogue as a complete sentence.

In Your Own Words . . . . *Run-On Sentences*

TURN to **page 87** in your handbook and read the section on run-on sentences.
REWRITE the section in your own words: First write a sentence that explains
   what a run-on sentence is. Then make up your own example of a run-on.
   Then, show two ways to correct it.

Newswriting . . . . *Run-On Sentences*

FIND a very short article (two or three paragraphs) in a newspaper.
COPY the article, but combine several pairs of sentences to make run-on
   sentences. (See **page 87** in your handbook for an example.)
Now, TRADE papers with a classmate who has done the same thing. Correct
   each other's article. Try to use both ways of correcting run-ons that are
   explained on page 87.
Finally, COMPARE your corrected article to the original article. How is it
   different?

And so on, and so on . . . . *Rambling Sentences*

FIND a very short news article (two or three paragraphs) in a newspaper.
   COPY the article onto a sheet of paper, leaving out all the end punctuation
   and initial capital letters. Add the word "and" in each place where a
   sentence ended. In other words, make the article into one long, rambling
   sentence.
Now TRADE papers with a classmate who has done the same thing.
   CORRECT each other's rambling sentences. If you need help, see **page 87**
   in your handbook.
Finally, COMPARE your corrected sentences with the original article. Your
   sentences don't have to match the article exactly, as long as they are
   correct and the meaning is clear.

Get it together. . . . . *Combining Sentences*

COMBINE each of the following pairs of sentences into one sentence. After each new sentence, write which rule for combining sentences you used. (The rules are listed and explained on **pages 90-93** in your handbook.) One example is shown below.

1. Marcy sent some valentines. Mark sent some valentines. **Marcy and Mark sent some valentines. (Use a compound subject.)**

2. The movie was long. The movie made me cry. *The movie was long and made me cry. (Use a compound verb.)*

3. Rahim got a new bike. It is red. *Rahim got a new, red bike. (Use a series of words.)*

4. My mother runs marathons. My mother swims laps. *My mother runs marathons and swims laps. (Use a compound verb.)*

5. My parents are going to France. I'm not going with them. *My parents are going to France, but I'm not going with them. (Use a conjunction.)*

6. My parents are flying to France. They're flying on a wide-body jet. *My parents are flying to France on a wide-body jet. (Use a prepositional phrase.)*

Understanding Our Language Minilessons

What am I? . . . . *Identifying Concrete Nouns*

COMPOSE "What Am I" riddles about 2-3 objects in your classroom.

Example: *I have a mouth and silver teeth that fall out everywhere. What am I? (answer: Stapler)*

SHARE your riddles with a classmate and listen to his or hers.

LIST all the riddle answers on the lines below. (See handbook **page 375** for an explanation of abstract and concrete nouns.) LABEL each noun "abstract" or "concrete." What have you discovered?

stapler	*concrete*

Just My Type

READ the essay "Why My Family Recycles Newspapers" on **page 76** in your handbook. Then USE **page 376** in your handbook to help you.

LABEL the 10 nouns in the first paragraph of the essay. The first one is done for you.

1. **family (object of preposition)**

2. *newspaper (direct object)*

3. *sister (subject)*

4. *parents (direct object)*

5. *recycling (direct object)*

6. *school (object of preposition)*

7. *newspapers (direct object)*

8. *paper (object of preposition)*

9. *newspapers (direct object)*

10. *environment (direct object)*

Special Challenge: WRITE your own sentences about recycling. EXCHANGE sentences with a partner and LABEL each noun.

Family Reunion . . . . *Relative Pronouns*

READ about relative pronouns on **page 379** in your handbook.

FIND the list of relative pronouns.

WRITE two or three sentences about one of your favorite relatives.

USE relative pronouns to help you share some interesting details about your cousin, uncle, grandmother, aunt, etc. You can have fun with this exercise; however, you don't want to embarrass anyone!

Mirror Image . . . . *Intensive and Reflexive Pronouns*

Intensive and reflexive pronouns work like mirrors in a sentence. See **page 379** in your handbook for examples and a list of intensive and reflexive pronouns.

CHOOSE one of the pronouns listed.

WRITE two sentences: one in which the pronoun is intensive and one in which it is reflexive.

ASK yourself what noun or pronoun your intensive or reflexive pronoun refers to in each sentence.

Special Challenge: TAKE turns reading your sentences for the class.

Lost and Found . . . . *Person of a Pronoun*

LIST all of the things you might find in the school's lost-and-found department.

CHOOSE two or three of these items and give them an opportunity to tell how they feel about being in the lost-and-found.

USE the first-person plural point of view. (That means you will be using the word *we* quite often.) See **page 378** of your handbook.

Name-Dropper . . . . *Using Irregular Verbs*

REVIEW the list of irregular verbs in your handbook on **page 382**.

FIND two irregular verbs that begin with the first letter in your first or last name. (If that doesn't work, use the name of a friend or family member.)

WRITE three crazy sentences for each verb by completing the sentence starters below. (Make sure that you use the correct form of the verb.)

1. *Yesterday, I* _____

_____

2. *I have* _____

_____

3. *I will* _____

_____

Sentence Ladder 1 . . . . *Adjectives*

START a sentence ladder with the following pattern.

The
spotted
little

dog waited in the
warm
yellow

car.

WRITE the above sentence on your paper.
THINK OF as many adjectives as possible to replace those in the boxes.
WRITE the replacements in a row of boxes under the adjectives "spotted" and
   "warm." (Keep going as long as you can.) SHARE your results with a partner.

Sentence Ladder 2 . . . . *Adverbs*

CREATE a sentence ladder by changing the adverb as many times as you can
   in each of the following sentences.

1. The motorcycle goes
fast.

2. I run
ahead.

USE different forms of the adverb when it is possible. *Example:* fast (positive),
   faster (comparative), fastest (superlative)

It's under the . . . , next to . . . . *Prepositions*

Have you ever had someone give you directions that sound more like a director directing an actor in a movie?

For Example: "Now go <u>into</u> the bedroom. <u>Against</u> the far wall, <u>next to</u> the window, you see the tall dresser. Open the top drawer <u>on</u> the left . . . "

WRITE specific directions for how to find something in a room at home, at school, or in another place that's very familiar to you.
As you write, USE a lot of prepositions. (See handbook **page 386.**)
TRADE papers. Can your partner visualize (see) what you're describing?
  The team that uses the most prepositions accurately wins!

Both . . . and . . . . *Conjunctions*

READ about correlative conjunctions in your handbook on **page 387.**
Then WRITE as many sentences as you can that use the correlative conjunctions "both, and." Here are some examples to get you started:

  Both Jose *and* I can wiggle our ears.

  Both girls *and* boys like to act funky.

SELECT your favorite sentences.
ARRANGE them as a poem titled "Both . . . and . . ."

Categories . . . . *Parts of Speech Overview*

CREATE a table with five spaces across and five spaces down. Down the side
WRITE five letters; across the top WRITE names of five parts of speech.
Then FILL IN the table with as many words as you can that correspond to
the letters and the parts of speech. Or, you may use the chart below.
ADD five more letters and exchange charts with a partner.
Special Challenge: THINK of ways to make this activity into a game. Or do
this as a timed activity.

	noun	adverb	preposition	verb	adjective
b	*box*	*badly*	*before*	*brushed*	*blue*
p					
d					
f					
o					

Check-It-Out Daily Sentences

The Check-It-Out Daily Sentences in this section of the SourceBook come in two different varieties. The focused sentences help students concentrate on one proofreading skill at a time. The proofreading sentences provide two or three different types of errors for students to correct.

Focused Sentences

● **End Punctuation**

Did you know there is one male calico cat for every 300,000 females ?

● **End Punctuation**

Heat makes you sleepy in the afternoon and restless at night .

● **End Punctuation**

Oh no, that plane is going to crash !

● **End Punctuation**

Why are all the Yellow Freight Company's trucks orange ?

● **End Punctuation**

Watch out for that speeding car !

Focused Sentences

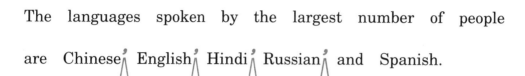

● **Commas (In a Series)**

The languages spoken by the largest number of people are Chinese, English, Hindi, Russian, and Spanish.

● **Commas (In a Series)**

The five most popular ice-cream flavors are vanilla, chocolate, Neapolitan, chocolate chip, and strawberry.

● **Commas (In a Series)**

According to a survey of historians, the best presidents of all time are Abraham Lincoln, George Washington, Franklin Roosevelt, Theodore Roosevelt, and Thomas Jefferson.

● **Commas (In a Series)**

Have you ever noticed a red, orange, silver, or beige tag on the back of Levi jeans?

● **Commas (In a Series)**

The word "facetiously" contains all of the vowels in the alphabet in order: a, e, i, o, u, and y.

122 *Check-It-Out Daily Sentences*

Focused Sentences

- ### Commas (Between Independent Clauses)

  A "Falling Rocks" sign means you are in an area where rocks could fall, but a "Fallen Rocks" sign means you should watch for rocks already on the road.

- ### Commas (Between Independent Clauses)

  A "Slow Children" sign does not mean the children in the area are slow, but it does mean drivers should slow down and watch carefully for children.

- ### Commas (Between Independent Clauses)

  <u>Tom and Jerry</u> is my least favorite cartoon show, so I only watch it if there's nothing else to do.

- ### Commas (Between Independent Clauses)

  President Franklin Roosevelt was crippled by polio, but the American public was not aware of how severe the crippling was.

- ### Commas (Between Independent Clauses)

  Not even the smartest scientists can figure out how the chubby bumblebee can fly, but it just goes ahead and flies anyway.

Focused Sentences

● **Commas (To Set Off Appositives)**

Hershey, Pennsylvania ⋀ home of the Hershey Chocolate Company ⋀ is called "Chocolate Town U.S.A."; Burlington, Wisconsin ⋀ home of Nestle's Chocolate Company ⋀ is called "Chocolate City U.S.A."

● **Commas (To Set Off Appositives)**

The Chicago Bears ⋀ National Football League champions of 1947 ⋀ played the college all-stars at Soldier Field ⋀ a huge stadium in Chicago.

● **Commas (To Set Off Appositives)**

A record crowd of 112,376 football fans watched the Houston Oilers beat the Dallas Cowboys ⋀ 1994 Super Bowl champions ⋀ in Mexico City on August 15.

● **Commas (To Set Off Appositives)**

Paul Anderson ⋀ the strongest man in the world ⋀ once lifted a table with six people on top of it.

● **Commas (To Set Off Appositives)**

Paul Anderson ⋀ 1956 Olympic weight lifter ⋀ won a gold medal for lifting 6,270 pounds.

Focused Sentences

● **Commas (To Set Off Long Phrases and Clauses)**

Early in the 1974 baseball season, Hank Aaron broke Babe Ruth's record by hitting his 715th home run.

● **Commas (To Set Off Long Phrases and Clauses)**

Even though some people think it was named after a baseball legend, the Baby Ruth candy bar was actually named after President Cleveland's oldest daughter, Ruth.

● **Commas (To Set Off Long Phrases and Clauses)**

When airplane pilots fly in an easterly direction, they fly at an odd-numbered altitude such as 29,000 feet.

● **Commas (To Set Off Long Phrases and Clauses)**

Flying at the even-numbered altitude of 30,000 feet, we knew we were headed west.

● **Commas (To Set Off Long Phrases and Clauses)**

As the fall winds blow the last leaves from the trees, the bears of northern Wisconsin begin looking for a good place to sleep.

Focused Sentences

● **Semicolon**

The United States has actually had a "King" living in the White House ⁀; President Gerald Ford's birth name before he was adopted was Leslie Lynch King, Jr.

● **Semicolon**

The very first Olympic Games took place in 776 B.C. at the foot of Mt. Olympus in Greece ⁀; the first modern Olympic Games were held in 1896 in Athens, Greece.

● **Semicolon**

The great Chicago fire of 1871 lasted 27 hours ⁀; it destroyed 17,450 buildings and killed 250 people.

● **Semicolon**

The Chisholm Trail runs between San Antonio and Abilene ⁀; many "real" cowboys herded cattle along that trail in 1871.

● **Semicolon**

Blowtorches of today can heat objects to over 14,000 degrees Fahrenheit ⁀; diamonds will actually burn at that temperature!

Focused Sentences

- **Hyphen**

  My well ᴧmeaning mother makes me take some

  nasty ᴧtasting cough medicine at the first sign of a cold.

- **Dash**

  Captain James T. Kirk of <u>Star Trek</u> fame has an uncommon

  middle name ᴧTiberius.

- **Dash**

  The first English author to receive the Nobel Prize for

  literature ᴧthis isn't surprising ᴧwas Rudyard Kipling in 1907.

- **Hyphen**

  Long ᴧplaying records (you know, those old ᴧfashioned albums

  your grandparents have) were invented by Peter Goldmark.

- **Dash**

  In 1867, a place where poor immigrant workers labored too

  hard and too long received a fitting name ᴧthe sweatshop.

Focused Sentences

● **Apostrophes**

Because singer Frank Sinatras *Sinatra's* eyes are a beautiful blue color, he is called Ol *Ol'* Blue Eyes by his fans.

● **Apostrophes**

All of the bicycles *bicycles'* horns out at the bike rack were broken by vandals.

● **Apostrophes**

The soft tissue of peoples *people's* vocal cords shrinks with age, making mens *men's* voices higher and womens *women's* softer.

● **Apostrophes**

Nebraskas *Nebraska's* winter winds blow hard and cold.

● **Apostrophes**

The Ts *T's* burned into the steers *steers'* hides tell you which ranch they belong to.

Focused Sentences

CHECK IT OUT

● **Quotation Marks**

"Happy Birthday to You" was adapted from a song by Mildred J. and Patty Hill called "Good Morning to You."

● **Quotation Marks**

The landlord yelled up the stairs, "Tap dancing sounds too much like a demolition derby down here! Try ballet!"

● **Quotation Marks**

I think "Writing Fantasies" is one of the best chapters in my new handbook, and there's a lot of cool stuff in "The Student Almanac," too!

● **Quotation Marks**

The phrase "passing the buck" was first written down by Mark Twain; it seems that poker players used to pass an object called a "buck" to the next dealer.

● **Quotation Marks**

The slang expression "ain't" dates back to King Charles II of England who used it as a substitute for "am not" or "are not."

Focused Sentences

● Italics (Underlining)

The three bears from the book <u>The Three Bears</u> must have liked porridge.

● Italics (Underlining)

The Marx Brothers starred in comic movies like <u>A Night at the Opera</u>.

● Italics (Underlining)

The words <u>do your homework</u> do not mean "Go ahead. Watch another episode of <u>Gilligan's Island</u>."

● Italics (Underlining)

The Marshmallow's latest record, <u>Soft Sugar</u>, is already a big hit.

● Italics (Underlining)

The Spanish word <u>hacienda</u> means a "large estate or plantation."

130   *Check-It-Out Daily Sentences*

Focused Sentences

● **Capitalization**

Mercury, the closest planet to the sun, is a little
                    E
larger than /earth's moon.

● **Capitalization**

                    T   R
The region of /transylvania is a real place in /romania.

● **Capitalization**

              E
Mount /everest is the highest mountain in the world, but it
                                                              M
is only 44 feet higher than K2, which is also called /mount
G   A
/godwin /austen.

● **Capitalization**

          C
The /chinese language is spoken by the most people in the
W   E
/World, but /english is the most widespread language.

● **Capitalization**

            B   K   H
Brad says /burger /king and /hardee's restaurants have the best
                                                          J
fries on the planet, but he's never tasted the food at /juicy
L
/lucy's truck stop.

Focused Sentences

● **Plurals**

The man at the corner stand sells ~~balloones~~ *balloons*, ~~boxs~~ *boxes* of candy, and ~~bunchs~~ *bunches* of flowers.

● **Plurals**

Henry VIII had six ~~wifes~~ *wives*. One of his ~~childs~~ *children* became a famous queen.

● **Plurals**

~~Monkies~~ *Monkeys* can chatter and howl, filling the jungle with ~~echos~~ *echoes* of their noise.

● **Plurals**

~~Elephantes~~ *Elephants*, whales, and ~~cowes~~ *cows* have ~~calfs~~ *calves* that require much care.

● **Plurals**

~~Soloes~~ *Solos* are played by one musician, duets by two, and ~~trioes~~ *trios* by three.

Focused Sentences

CHECK IT OUT

● **Numbers**

There are over three ~~and a half~~ *3.5 billion* billion chickens in the

world — plenty of drumsticks to go around!

● **Numbers**

Twenty
~~20~~ of my classmates made the honor roll last quarter; that's

90
~~ninety~~ percent of the class!

● **Numbers**

113
A female blue whale measuring one ~~hundred and thirteen~~ feet

in length is the largest animal ever seen alive.

● **Numbers**

1993
In ~~nineteen ninety-three~~ the Clinton family moved to

1600
~~Sixteen Hundred~~ Pennsylvania Avenue, Washington, D.C.

20006
~~Two Zero Zero Zero Six.~~

● **Numbers**

4 *5* *40*
Skip chapters ~~four~~ and ~~five~~ for now, but read pages ~~forty~~

41
and ~~forty-one~~ in chapter 6 for tomorrow.

Focused Sentences

● **Using the Right Word**

I've heard ~~tails~~ *tales* of the ~~see's~~ *sea's* rage that would turn ~~you're~~ *your* hair white!

● **Using the Right Word**

If you ~~poor~~ *pour* all of the lemonade into ~~you're~~ *your* glass, ~~their~~ *there* will be nothing left for me to drink.

● **Using the Right Word**

A storm window keeps the warm ~~heir~~ *air* in ~~you're~~ *your* house ~~wear~~ *where* it belongs.

● **Using the Right Word**

It ~~seams~~ *seems* that the piccolo players always ~~set~~ *sit* next to the flutists in ~~a~~ *an* orchestra.

● **Using the Right Word**

Little Ralphy untied all the ~~nots~~ *knots* he'd tied in the maid's apron strings, so she gave him ~~a~~ *an* extra ~~peace~~ *piece* of cake afterward.

Focused Sentences

(Answers may vary.)

- ## Combining Sentences

  The class of animals called Arachnida includes spiders.
  This class includes scorpions. It includes ticks as well.

  The class of animals called Arachnida includes spiders, scorpions, and ticks.

- ## Combining Sentences

  The piece of amber contains a fossilized dragonfly.
  The piece of amber is golden. It is on the professor's desk.

  The golden piece of amber on the professor's desk contains a fossilized dragonfly.

- ## Combining Sentences

  The Swiss Alps are cut by many deep valleys.
  The valleys contain pretty towns and villages.

  The Swiss Alps are cut by many deep valleys, which contain pretty towns and villages.

- ## Combining Sentences

  Greenland is the largest island on earth.
  Greenland was discovered in 982 by Eric the Red.

  Greenland is the largest island on earth and was discovered in 982 by Eric the Red.

- ## Combining Sentences

  Canoeing on rivers in the spring can be dangerous.
  Sudden rainstorms can cause flash flooding.

  Canoeing on rivers in the spring can be dangerous because sudden rainstorms can cause flash flooding.

Focused Sentences

● **Subject-Verb Agreement**

An African black mamba snake ~~have~~ *has* been clocked slithering at 30 miles an hour.

● **Subject-Verb Agreement**

Sidewinder rattlesnakes actually ~~moves~~ *move* by jumping sideways along the ground.

● **Subject-Verb Agreement**

Either the mamba or the blue racer ~~are~~ *is* poisonous, but I can't remember which one.

● **Subject-Verb Agreement**

Chocolate and vanilla ~~remains~~ *remain* the favorite ice-cream flavors.

● **Subject-Verb Agreement**

The highest bridge in the world ~~were~~ *was* built 1,053 feet above Royal Gorge in Colorado.

Proofreading Sentences

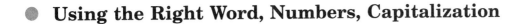

CHECK IT OUT

● **Using the Right Word, Numbers, Capitalization**

The oldest letter of the alphabet is the letter "O," dating
back ~~two~~ *to* the year ~~three thousand~~ *3,000* ~~b.c.~~ *B.C.*

● **Subject-Verb Agreement, Commas (In a Series)**

Our language ~~are~~ *is* always changing because of the way we

talk, write, and use words from day to day.

● **Using the Right Word, Contractions, Double Negative**

Some
~~Sum~~ slang words used in the 1960's ~~arent~~ *aren't* ~~never~~ used much

anymore.
(Answers may vary.)

● **Numbers, Using the Right Word, Run-On Sentence**

I
Calligraphy is the art of beautiful handwriting. ~~it~~ developed

an   *2,000*
into ~~a~~ art form more than ~~two thousand~~ years ago.
(Answers may vary.)

● **Commas (To Set Off Appositives), Capitalization**

R
Latin, the language of the ~~r~~oman Empire, is the foundation

E
of the ~~e~~nglish language.

Proofreading Sentences

Animal Crackers 1

● **Possessives, Using the Right Word**

hummingbird's   *for*

A ~~hummingbirds~~ bill works like a straw ~~four~~ sucking nectar

from a flower.

● **Plurals, Commas (In a Series)**

                            crickets   *salamanders*

Certain kinds of bats, ~~cricketes~~, and ~~salamanderes~~ live in caves.

● **Adjectives (Comparative), Possessives, Using the Right Word**

    giraffe's   *than*   *human's*

A ~~giraffes~~ neck has no more bones ~~then~~ a ~~humans~~ — the

bones are simply ~~more~~ larger.

● **Possessives, Using the Right Word**

Parrots'   *to*

~~Parrots~~ bills work like nutcrackers ~~too~~ open seeds and nuts.

● **Subject-Verb Agreement, Sentence Fragment**

(Answers may vary.)

                                        is

Either the emu baby or the kangaroo baby ~~are~~ called a joey.

I c

~~C~~an't remember.

138 *Check-It-Out Daily Sentences*

Proofreading Sentences

Animal Crackers 2

- ## Commas (To Set Off Long Phrases and Clauses), Using the Right Word

  it's
  When a horse and a donkey have a foal ‸ it's called a mule.

- ## Commas (Between Independent Clauses), Using the Right Word

  tail
  The kangaroo has a long, thick tale ‸ and this helps the

  animal balance while leaping.

- ## Irregular Verbs, Pronoun/Antecedent Agreement, Contractions

  saw
  If you ever sawed a picture of a pike (a kind of fish), I

  you'd   *it looks*
  think you'd agree they look really mean.

- ## Subject-Verb Agreement, Plurals, Double Negative

  has   *wolves*
  There have never been no documented proof of healthy wolfs

  attacking human beings.

  (Answers may vary.)

- ## Hyphens, Pronoun/Antecedent Agreement, Using the Right Word

  -    -   *their*   *they*
  Two ‸ year ‸ old bears are as large as there parents when it

  leave
  leaves home.

Proofreading Sentences

Maps, Maps, Maps 1

- ## End Punctuation, Capitalization

  The oldest map of the _W_/World is a clay tablet from Babylon made around 600 B.C./

- ## Capitalization, Using the Right Word

  The base of the _G_/great _P_/pyramid of _G_/giza is a perfect square with the _four_/~~for~~ sides resting on exact _n_/North-_s_/South and _e_/East-_w_/West lines.

- ## Commas (To Set Off Appositives), Parentheses

  Mount Everest, the tallest mountain in the world, still grows at a rate of one centimeter (that's .394 inches) every year.

- ## Commas (To Set Off Appositives and in Dates)

  On May 28, 1953, Sir Edmund Hillary, an explorer from New Zealand, and Tenzing Norkay, a guide from Nepal, became the first people to reach the top of Mount Everest.

- ## Using the Right Word, Commas (To Set Off Long Phrases), Capitalization

  According to the _U_/united _S_/states _G_/geological _S_/survey, every year ~~they're~~ _there are_ over ~~an~~ _a_ million little earthquakes around the world.

Proofreading Sentences

Maps, Maps, Maps 2

● **Subject-Verb Agreement, Using the Right Word**

The first true cities ~~was~~ *were* the ~~capitols~~ *capitals* of early civilizations,

such as Ur in Mesopotamia.

● **Numbers, Capitalization, End Punctuation**

The ~~p~~*P*yramids of ~~g~~*G*iza are one of the ~~7~~ *seven* wonders of the

world*;* ~~d~~*D*o you know what the other ~~6~~ *six* are and what they

have in common*?*

● **Parentheses, Irregular Verbs**

American explorer Richard E. Byrd *(*1888-1957*)* ~~becomed~~ *became* the

first person to fly over the North Pole in 1926.

● **Commas (In Dates), Using the Right Word, Possessives**

On July 11*,* 1969*,* Neil Armstrong became the first man ~~too~~ *to*

walk on the ~~moons~~ *moon's* surface.

● **Subject-Verb Agreement, Possessives, Run-On Sentence**

(Answer may vary.)

Robert E. Peary and Roald Amundsen ~~was~~ *were* the first explorers

to arrive at the ~~earth~~ *earth's* poles*.* Peary went north in 1909, and

Amundsen went south in 1911.

Proofreading Sentences

Maps, Maps, Maps 3

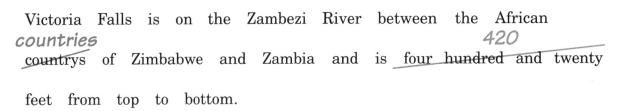

● Plurals, Numbers

Victoria Falls is on the Zambezi River between the African

countries
~~countrys~~ of Zimbabwe and Zambia and is four ~~hundred~~ *420* and twenty

feet from top to bottom.

● Capitalization, Numbers

G ~~~~ *n*
The ~~g~~reat Barrier Reef off the ~~N~~ortheast coast of Australia is

1,200
~~one thousand and two hundred~~ miles of beautifully colored coral.

● Capitalization, Numbers

T
The Sears ~~t~~ower is the tallest building in the world with

110 *1500*
~~one hundred and ten~~ stories that rise almost ~~fifteen hundred~~ feet

443 *C*
~~(four hundred and forty-three~~ meters) above the streets of ~~c~~hicago.

● Subject-Verb Agreement, Adjectives (Superlative)

live *highest*
The Uru people ~~lives~~ on the ~~most high~~ island in the world in

the middle of Lake Titicaca in South America.

● Capitalization, Using the Right Word

Scientists have found fish skeletons in the middle of the Sahara
Desert *there* *there*
~~dessert~~, which indicates that once ~~their~~ was an ocean ~~their~~.

Proofreading Sentences

Maps, Maps, Maps 4

● **Possessives, Using the Right Word**

Sweden's
~~Swedens~~ capital city of Stockholm is built on an island

to   *by*
attached ~~too~~ the mainland ~~buy~~ many bridges.

● **Using the Right Word, Capitalization**

its
The country of Brazil moved ~~it's~~ capitol from the coastal

B
city of Rio de Janeiro inland to the new city of ~~b~~rasilia.

● **Adjectives (Superlative), Commas (To Set Off Appositives)**

worst
The ~~baddest~~ criminals of England used to be sent to

Tasmania ‸ an island off the coast of Australia.

● **Capitalization, Numbers, Plurals, Parallelism**

three S   *countries*
The ~~3~~ ~~s~~outh American ~~countrys~~ of Guyana, Suriname, and

cities
French Guiana are north of Brazil, have port ~~citys~~ for

border   *O*
capitals, and each ~~country~~ ~~borders~~ the Atlantic ~~o~~cean.

● **Italics (Underlining), Capitalization**

L
The word "peninsula" comes from the ~~l~~atin paene for "almost"

and insulae for "island."

Proofreading Sentences

Colors, Signs, and Symbols 1

● **Commas (To Set Off Long Phrases and Clauses),
Using the Right Word**

When riding your bike , extend you're *your* left arm straight out
to
too signal a left turn.

● **Commas (To Set Off Long Phrases and Clauses),
Subject-Verb Agreement, Using the Right Word**

right
To signal a write turn on your bike , extend your left arm out
bend
and bends it up at the elbow with your palm forward.

● **Subject-Verb Agreement, Using the Right Word**

signals *is*
The director of a television show signal that time are running
by *an*
out buy swirling a index finger around in a circle.

● **Possessives, Subject-Verb Agreement**

director's *indicates*
A tap of a finger on a television directors nose indicate that

the performer or announcer is right on time.

● **Commas (To Set Off Long Phrases and Clauses),
Subject-Verb Agreement**

When a television director rubs together the index finger and
is
thumb of both hands , the performer or announcer on stage are

being signaled to slow down.

Proofreading Sentences

Colors, Signs, and Symbols 2

● **Possessives, Plurals, Parentheses**

The different patterns and ~~colores~~ *colors* of ~~Scotlands~~ *Scotland's* kilts ∧ skirts ∧ ( )

represent different clans, or ~~familys~~ *families*.

● **Possessives, Combining Sentences** *(Answers may vary.)*

~~Brides~~ *Brides'* dresses are often white/ ~~T~~hat color has symbolized *since t*

joy for many years.

● **Quotation Marks, Capitalization**

" Sequoyah created a written language for the ~~c~~herokee people *C*

in 1821, " said ~~m~~rs. ~~h~~enning. *M* *H*

● **Capitalization, Commas (To Set Off Interruptions), Possessives**

Uncle ~~s~~am ∧ in case you don't know ∧ was a real person *S*

whose famous picture was used on the u.s ~~armys~~ *U.S. Army's*

enlistment posters.

● **Using the Right Word, Subject-Verb Agreement, Commas (To Set Off Appositives)**

Putting ~~you're~~ index finger and thumb together to make *your*

∧ "O" ~~are~~ a ~~weigh~~ of saying OK ∧ which means "all right." *an* *is* *way*

Proofreading Sentences

Colors, Signs, and Symbols 3

● **Colon, Commas (In a Series)**

The acronym ROY G. BIV stands for each of the colors of the rainbow ⋀: red ⋀, orange ⋀, yellow ⋀, green ⋀, blue ⋀, indigo ⋀, and violet.

● **Using the Right Word, Commas (To Set Off Interruptions)**

Ordinary white light ⋀, which can be separated ~~buy~~ *by* a prism ⋀, is ~~maid~~ *made* up of all the colors of the rainbow.

● **Commas (To Set Off Appositives), Contractions, Using the Right Word**

Ultraviolet is a light beyond violet ⋀, the last color of the spectrum; ultraviolet radiation ~~cant~~ *can't* be ~~scene~~ *seen*.

● **Commas (Between Independent Clauses), Contractions, Subject-Verb Agreement**

Objects ~~reflects~~ *reflect* different parts of the light spectrum ⋀, and ~~thats~~ *that's* why we see colors.

● **Using the Right Word, Run-On Sentence**
(Answers may vary.)

A laser beam is photons of light traveling in the same direction ⋀. ~~s~~ *S*uch a beam can be powerful enough to burn a ~~whole~~ *hole* in ~~medal~~ *metal*.

Proofreading Sentences

Colors, Signs, and Symbols 4

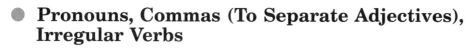

- **Pronouns, Commas (To Separate Adjectives), Irregular Verbs**

  The common *,* everyday handshake ~~begun~~ *began* when men wanted to

  show each other ~~them~~ *they* did not have weapons in their hands.

- **Subject-Verb Agreement, Run-On Sentence** *(Answers may vary.)*

  You ~~has~~ *have* to identify many traffic signs when you ride a bike *;*

  the stop sign and the yield sign are two important ones.

- **Commas (In a Series), Parentheses**

  The police *,* the military *,* the FBI *(*Federal Bureau of Investigation*),*

  and other organizations use fingerprints to identify people.

- **Capitalization, Commas (In a Series)**

  In his paintings, Pablo *P*icasso used different shapes to

  represent people *,* animals *,* things *,* and ideas.

- **Commas (To Set Off Appositives), Capitalization, Subject-Verb Agreement**

  Leonardo da Vinci *,* one of the greatest *I*talian painters *,* ~~were~~ *was*

  also interested in many areas of science.

Proofreading Sentences

U.S. History 1

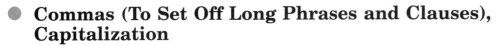

- **Commas (To Set Off Long Phrases and Clauses), Capitalization**

  Once the new *A*/american government was installed in 1789 , George Washington was sworn in as the first *P*/president.

- **Possessives, Irregular Verbs, Capitalization**

  The Civil *W*/war ~~begun~~ *began* in 1861 when the ~~Confederate's~~ *Confederates* opened fire upon Fort Sumter.

- **Capitalization, Commas (In Dates)**

  The *C*/civil *W*/war ended at *A*/appomattax *C*/court *H*/house on April 9 , 1865.

- **Irregular Verbs, Capitalization, Hyphens**

  Rioting ~~taked~~ *took* place when an African-American student named James Meredith enrolled at the *U*/university of Mississippi in 1962.

- **Numbers, Commas (To Set Off Long Phrases and Clauses), Hyphens**

  Upon entering the University of Georgia in 1962 , Charlayne Hunter-Gault became the first African-American student there in ~~one hundred seventy-five~~ *175* years.

Proofreading Sentences

U.S. History 2

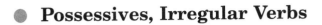

● **Possessives, Irregular Verbs**

Uncle ~~Sams~~ *Sam's* picture was first ~~drawed~~ *drawn* by cartoonist

Thomas Nast.

● **Possessives, Using the Right Word, Colon**

Thomas Nast also drew the ~~mane~~ *main* political party symbols : the

~~Democrats~~ *Democrats'* donkey and the ~~Republicans~~ *Republicans'* elephant.

● **Commas (In Addresses), Capitalization**

The first United States Congress met in *P*princeton , *N*new *J*jersey ,

not in Washington , D.C.

● **Capitalization, Commas (In Dates), Using the Right Word**

President Lincoln issued the *E*emancipation *P*proclamation on

*S*september 22 , 1862, and it took ~~affect~~ *effect* on *J*january 1 , 1863.

● **Capitalization, Using the Right Word**

During the *R*roaring *T*twenties, women ~~which~~ *who* cut ~~there~~ *their* hair

short and danced the Charleston were called "flappers."

Proofreading Sentences

Science and Inventions 1

- **Subject-Verb Agreement, Capitalization, Commas (To Set Off Appositives)**

         C

  Marie ~~c~~urie, one of the first noted female scientists, ~~were~~ *was* born

   P

  in ~~p~~oland in 1867.

- **Capitalization, Run-On Sentence, Abbreviations**

  (Answers may vary.)

                                       m

  Elizabeth Blackwell graduated from ~~M~~edical school in 1849; she

                        United States

  was the first woman in the U.S. to earn a medical degree.

- **Colon, Capitalization, Possessives**

                   earth's   *P*

  Scientists divide the ~~earths~~ history into four eras: ~~p~~recambrian,

  P   *M*   *C*

  ~~p~~aleozoic, ~~m~~esozoic, ~~c~~enozoic.

- **Subject-Verb Agreement, Possessives, Numbers**

  Scientists   *seven*   *were*

  ~~Scientist's~~ believe that the earth's ~~7~~ continents ~~was~~ once attached.

- **Quotation Marks, Commas (In a Series), Capitalization**

                                      " *p*

  One definition of the word "~~P~~recipitation" refers to hail, mist, rain,

  sleet, or snow.

Proofreading Sentences

Science and Inventions 2

● **Commas (Between Independent Clauses), Using the Right Word**

Kinetic energy is the energy of moving things ⌃ and potential

                                   that

energy is energy ~~who~~ could be used.

● **Capitalization, Possessives, Commas (In a Series)**

           W   *South's*

George ⁄washington Carver greatly helped the ~~souths~~ economy

by improving peanuts ⌃ soybeans ⌃ and sweet potatoes.

● **Subject-Verb Agreement, Using the Right Word**

                       right   *make*   *for*

Growth hormones in the ~~write~~ places ~~makes~~ it possible ~~four~~

              to

a plant ~~two~~ bend toward the light.

● **Run-On Sentence, Using the Right Word**

(Answers may vary.)

                                                its

A firefly lights up when the air tubes in ~~it's~~ stomach are

           by   *It's*

filled ~~buy~~ oxygen and a pigment of fat ⌃ ~~its~~ not magic or

electricity.

● **Contractions, Using the Right Word, End Punctuation, Plurals**

  Don't   *your*   *already knows*

~~Dont~~ you think ~~you're~~ science teacher ~~all ready~~ ~~nose~~ that a

            monkeys   *?*

group of ~~monkies~~ is a band ⁄

Proofreading Sentences

Science and Inventions 3

● **Using the Right Word, Numbers**

desert

A ~~dessert~~ is any area of the earth that gets ~~fewer~~ *less* than ~~1~~ *one*

inch of rainfall every year.

● **Commas (To Set Off Long Phrases and Clauses), Possessives, Adjectives (Comparative)**

ocean's   *colder*

The farther you go below the ~~oceans~~ surface ⌄ the ~~more~~ cold

and saltier it gets.

● **Using the Right Word, Adverbs (Comparative)**

than

Sound travels ~~more~~ better and ~~more~~ faster in water ~~then~~ in air

because the liquid molecules are closer together.

● **Pronoun/Antecedent Agreement, Using the Right Word**

way *they*

Certain supernovas, or superstars, flare up in a big ~~weigh;~~ ~~it~~

suns

may reach the brilliance of 200 million ~~sons~~!

● **Plurals, Parallelism**

Potatoes

~~Potatos~~ consist mainly of starch, protein, and ~~they~~ ~~have~~ water

~~in~~ them.

Proofreading Sentences

Literature and Life 1

- **Subject-Verb Agreement, Sentence Fragment, Italics (Underlining Titles)** *(Answers may vary.)*

  My friend and I ~~wants~~ *want* to see the movie <u>King Kong</u>, a story about a big, hairy ape. ~~Actually~~ *The ape actually* attacks New York City!

- **Capitalization, Possessives**

  Just ~~t~~*T*ell ~~m~~*M*e ~~w~~*W*hen ~~w~~*W*e're ~~d~~*D*ead and ~~h~~*H*ot and ~~c~~*C*old ~~s~~*S*ummer are the ~~childrens~~ *children's* favorite books.

- **Using the Right Word, Adjectives (Comparative), Capitalization**

  Anwar and Sumo are ~~more~~ better names for kittens ~~then~~ *than* the two most popular ones, ~~t~~*T*iger and ~~s~~*S*amantha.

- **Rambling Sentence, Numbers** *(Answers may vary.)*

  I don't want to wear mink, and I could wear my wool coat instead, and ~~and~~ *D*id you know that ~~forty~~ *40* mink had to die for that coat?

- **Pronoun/Antecedent Agreement, Commas (In Direct Address)**

  Class, we will write panagrams today. ~~It is~~ *They are* sentences that use all the letters of the alphabet.

Proofreading Sentences

Literature and Life 2

- ### Capitalization, Commas (To Set Off Appositives)

  In 1933 *M*mickey *M*mouse received quite a few more fan letters

  than Shirley Temple⌃, the most popular living performer.

- ### Commas (To Set Off Appositives), Possessives, Italics (Underlining Titles)

  Theodor Geisel⌃, also known as Dr. Seuss⌃, wrote the wonderful

  children's
  childrens books <u>The Cat in the Hat</u> and <u>Green Eggs and Ham</u>.

- ### Italics (Underlining Titles), Numbers, Capitalization

  Robert *L*louis *S*stevenson wrote <u>The Strange Case of *D*dr. Jekyll

  M *three*
  and *M*mr. Hyde in 3 days.</u>

- ### Using the Right Word, Capitalization

  It's
  Its true that *M*mark *T*twain liked *writing* righting in bed and produced

  quite *there*
  quiet a few chapters their in pure comfort.

- ### Commas (In Dates), Capitalization, Irregular Verbs

  J *B J* *became*
  On june 22, 1990⌃, billy joel becomed the first *r*Rock 'n' *r*Roll

  artist to perform in Yankee Stadium.

Proofreading Sentences

Literature and Life 3

- **Using the Right Word, Numbers, Capitalization**

  pour   *F*   *L*   *would*
  If you were to poor a bowl of fruit loops, wood you get
  three   *five*
  3, four, or 5 flavors?

- **Capitalization, Using the Right Word**

  to   *B*
  In the summer I like going too the store for breyer's ice
  G
  cream and graf's root beer.

- **Italics (Underlining Titles), Capitalization, Run-On Sentence**

  (Answers may vary.)   *W*   *C*   *I*
  You should read The Moonstone by wilkie collins, it's about

  a diamond.

- **Using the Right Word, Capitalization, Contractions**

  N   *you'll meet*
  If you read The Chronicles of narnia, youll meat the
  R
  character reepicheep.

- **Italics (Underlining Titles), Capitalization, Abbreviations**

  D   *S*
  The Lorax, written by dr seuss, is a tale about the

  conservation of our natural resources.

Proofreading Sentences

Literature and Life 4

● **Capitalization, Quotation Marks**

Our teacher asked, "Who was the Goddess of flowers in Roman Mythology—Diana, Flora, or Helen?"

● **Using the Right Word, Commas (To Set Off Long Phrases), Capitalization, Italics (Underlining Titles)**

In the novel The Prisoner of Zenda, king Rudolf rules an country called ruritania.

● **Commas (To Set Off Long Phrases), Capitalization, Italics (Underlining Titles)**

Besides alice's adventures in wonderland, Lewis Carroll wrote the hunting of the snark and a tangled tale.

● **Using the Right Word, Capitalization, Parallelism**

The hula hoop is named after that hawaiian dance in witch you sway your hips, keep your upper torso still, and then you move your arms and hands gently.

● **Capitalization, Rambling Sentence, Contractions**

(Answers may vary.)

Im glad I dont live in the stone age and, besides, I like the new fashions and all the modern conveniences and I'm also looking forward to driving a car.